THE NEW QUID REGULATIONS

THE CHANDOS SERIES ON THE FOOD INDUSTRY

in association with

THE BRITISH LIBRARY

The British Library is a great national institution and one of the most important libraries in the world. Its Science Reference and Information Service (SRIS) is a unique resource for the UK business and industry, government and academic communities, offering access to a wide range of literature, including the largest patent collection in the world and an increasing amount of material in electronic form.

Information inquirers from the food industry will find that SRIS holds much relevant material, whether they are looking for market assessments for particular types of products, the latest patents on food technology or research journals dealing with nutrition. For those who need help in finding information and those unable to visit the Library in person, there are specialised information services, free of charge for simple queries and competitively priced when dealing with more complex inquiries. SRIS also publishes a range of books and databases to help the user identify and evaluate information sources in particular scientific, technical and business subjects.

To find out more about SRIS' collections and specialist services, contact: SRIS Marketing and Public Relations, 25 Southampton Buildings, London WC2A 1AW (tel 0171-412 7959, fax 0171-412 7947, email sris-customer-services@bl.uk). During 1999 SRIS will be moving to the new British Library building at 96 Euston Road, London NW1 2DB.

To complement the services of SRIS, documents can be supplied to customers offsite via the Library's Document Supply Centre (DSC). The Centre provides the most comprehensive photocopy/loan service in the world and has unrivalled collections of journals, books, conference proceedings and theses, as well as the UK National Reports Collection.

For more information on DSC services telephone 01937-546060, fax 01937-546333 or email dsc-customer-services@bl.uk.

Anyone with an Internet connection can find out more about British Library services on http://www.bl.uk/ or you can access our catalogue on http://opac97.bl.uk/.

THE NEW QUID REGULATIONS

Practical Guidance on the New Regulations and Other Food Labelling Legislation

Catriona Crawford

Chandos Publishing (Oxford) Limited
in association with
The British Library

ISBN 1 902375 15 7

© C. Crawford, 1998

Chandos Publishing (Oxford) Limited
Chandos House
5 & 6 Steadys Lane
Stanton Harcourt
Oxford OX8 1RL
England

Tel: 01865 884447 Fax: 01865 884448

Printed in England

Contents

ACRONYMS

The following acronyms for certain well-known organisations have been used in the text:

COMA   Committee on Medical Aspects of Food Policy

EC   European Community

EU   European Union

FAC   Food Advisory Committee

LACOTS   Local Authorities Coordinating Body on Food and Trading Standards

MAFF   Ministry of Agriculture, Fisheries and Food

THE AUTHOR

The author was, until April 1996, Legislation Advisor to the Campden and Chorleywood Food Research Association.

Her early career was concerned with food research and food analysis. Food law has been an important factor throughout and became a full time preoccupation in 1989, when appointed Legislation Advisor.

Her previous posts included: Scientific Officer, Laboratory of the Government Chemist; Senior Scientist, Leatherhead Food Research Association; and Principal Scientific Officer, Flour Milling and Baking Research Association (which became part of the Campden and Chorleywood Food Research Association).

The author can be contacted through the publishers.

CHAPTER 1

Introduction

The Food Labelling Regulations 1996 came finally into effect on 1 July 1997 and introduced a number of changes to labelling law with which food manufacturers, processors and retailers must comply. More recently, *The Food Labelling (Amendment) Regulations 1998*, the so-called QUID regulations, were issued and came into force on 1 July 1998. The principal effect of these regulations is to require the quantity of certain ingredients to be indicated on the label. Although these requirements need not be complied with until 14 February 2000, the food industry will want to become fully aware of its new obligations at the earliest opportunity, so as to make preparations to meet them with the minimum of disruption and as soon as is convenient.

This guide is concerned with the legal requirements applying to the labelling of food for retail sale or for supply to restaurants and other caterers. Many of these requirements are laid down in *The Food Labelling Regulations 1996* and the 1998 amending regulations, but other legislation also imposes labelling obligations. It has therefore been necessary to take into account, for example, the weights and measures regulations, *The Food (Lot Marking) Regulations 1996* and *The Milk and Milk Products (Protection of Designations) Regulations 1990*. The additional labelling required by certain regulations relating to specific foods, such as *The Cocoa and Chocolate Products Regulations 1976*, has in most cases not been included, being beyond the scope of this book, as are the rules on price marking.

It seemed appropriate to include the advice provided by certain guidelines, in particular those on nutrition claims and on use of the word 'natural', based in both cases on recommendations made by the Food Advisory Committee. Although these guidelines have no statutory force, they are likely to be referred to by the enforcement authorities when deciding whether or not a labelling offence has been committed. The text also relies on guidance notes issued by the Ministry of Agriculture, Fisheries and

Food, an authoritative source of non-statutory information, invaluable in the interpretation of the law and for illustrative purposes.

The legislation is complex. An attempt has been made to present information in a simple and systematic form using a system of cross-referencing so as to aid easy reference. Nevertheless, much of the language used follows closely that of the regulations, since too much simplification can easily lead to misinterpretation.

The aim of the guide is to enable the busy manager or technician to gain an understanding of the many facets of UK food labelling law without the need to master the regulations themselves, which can be a daunting and difficult task requiring much time and effort. The text should provide a useful source of reference to all those who have an involvement with food labelling. It must be stressed, however, that this guide is not a legal document and that for definitive purposes, the legislation itself should be consulted.

The reader should be aware that, as with most of the legislation mentioned in this book, *The Food Labelling Regulations 1996* apply to England, Scotland and Wales while a separate but similar law applies to Northern Ireland.

Compliance with the provisions of *The Food Labelling Regulations* is in the interests of both the consumer and the food industry. It is an offence not to comply. Prosecutions for labelling offences may be brought under *The Food Labelling Regulations*, *The Food Safety Act* or *The Trade Descriptions Act*.

Section 15 of *The Food Safety Act* makes it an offence to display a label or publish an advertisement which falsely describes a food or is likely to mislead as to its nature, substance or quality. It is also an offence to sell food, the presentation of which is likely to mislead as to its nature, substance or quality.

Under the *Trade Descriptions Act* it is an offence to apply a false or misleading trade description to any goods.

Both acts make provision for a due diligence defence. This enables a defendant to be acquitted if they prove that they took all reasonable precautions and exercised all due diligence to avoid committing the offence.

A defence of deemed due diligence is available to retailers who can prove that the offence was the fault of someone else, that they had no reason to suspect that they were committing an offence and that, in the case of 'own label' products, they made reasonable checks on the food or reasonably relied on checks made by the supplier.

CHAPTER 2

Definitions

Precise definitions are necessary for a correct interpretation of the law. The following definitions all derive from *The Food Labelling Regulations* (apart from that for polyols which can be found in the MAFF Guidance Notes on *The Sweeteners in Food Regulations*). These definitions therefore apply for the purposes of *The Food Labelling Regulations* and whilst many of them are valid also within the context of other legislation, it is important to be aware that this is not necessarily the case.

2.1 **Additive** means any substance not normally consumed as a food in itself and not normally used as a characteristic ingredient of food, whether or not it has nutritive value, the intentional addition of which to a food for a technological purpose in the manufacture, processing, preparation, treatment, packaging, transport or storage of such a food results, or may be reasonably expected to result, in it or its by-products becoming directly or indirectly a component of such foods.

2.2 **Biscuits** includes wafers, rusks, oatcakes and matzos.

2.3 **Carbohydrate** means any carbohydrate which is metabolised in man and includes polyols (*see* 2.29).

2.4 **Catering establishment** means a restaurant, canteen, club, public house, school, hospital or similar establishment (including a vehicle or a fixed or mobile stall) where, in the course of a business, food is prepared for delivery to the ultimate consumer (*see* 2.45) and is ready for consumption without further preparation.

2.5   **Clotted cream** means cream which has been produced and separated by the scalding, cooling and skimming of milk or cream.

2.6   **Cream** means that part of cows' milk rich in fat which has been separated by skimming or otherwise and which is intended for sale for human consumption.

2.7   **Community controlled wine** means wine, grape must, sparkling wine, aerated sparkling wine, liqueur wine, semi-sparkling wine and aerated semi-sparkling wine.

2.8   **Confectionery product** means any item of chocolate confectionery or sugar confectionery.

2.9   **Disease** includes any injury, ailment or adverse condition, whether of body or mind.

2.10 **Edible ice** includes ice-cream, water ice and fruit ice, whether alone or in combination, and any similar food.

2.11 **Fancy confectionery product** means any confectionery product (*see* 2.8) in the form of a figure, animal, cigarette or egg or in any other fancy form.

2.12 **Fat**, in the context of nutrition labelling, means total lipids, and includes phospholipids.

2.13 **Flavouring** (used as a noun) means an additive consisting of material used or intended for use in or on food to impart odour, taste or both (provided that such material does not consist entirely of any edible substance (including herbs and spices) or product, intended for human consumption as such, with or without reconstitution, or any substance which has exclusively a sweet, sour or salt taste) and the components of which include at least one of the following: a flavouring substance (*see* 2.15); a flavouring preparation (*see* 2.14); a process flavouring (*see* 2.35); or a smoke flavouring (*see* 2.41).

2.14 **Flavouring preparation** means a product (other than a flavouring substance), whether concentrated or not, with flavouring properties, which is obtained by physical, enzymatic or microbiological processes from appropriate material of vegetable or animal origin.

2.15 **Flavouring substance** means a chemical substance with flavouring properties the chemical structure of which has been established by methods normally used among scientists and which is:

(a) obtained by physical, enzymatic or microbiological processes from appropriate material of vegetable or animal origin;

(b) either obtained by chemical synthesis or isolated by chemical processes and which is chemically identical to a substance naturally present in appropriate material of vegetable or animal origin; or

(c) obtained by chemical synthesis but not included under sub-paragraph (b) of this definition.

For the purposes of this definition and the definition of 'flavouring preparation':

(i) distillation and solvent extraction are regarded as included among types of physical process;

(ii) material of vegetable or animal origin is appropriate material of vegetable or animal origin if it either is raw or has been subjected to a process normally used in preparing food for human consumption and to no process other than one normally so used; and

(iii) drying, torrefaction and fermentation are included among the types of process normally so used to which sub-paragraph (ii) above refers.

2.16 **Flour confectionery** means any cooked food which is ready for consumption without further preparation (other than reheating), of which a characterising ingredient is ground cereal, including shortbread, sponges, crumpets, muffins, macaroons, ratafias, pastry and pastry cases, and also includes meringues, petits fours and uncooked pastry and pastry cases, but does not include bread, pizzas, biscuits, crispbread, extruded flat bread or any food containing a filling which has as an ingredient any cheese, meat, offal, fish, shellfish, vegetable protein material or microbial protein material.

2.17 **Food for a particular nutritional use** means a food intended for human consumption which, owing to its special composition or process of manufacture, is clearly distinguishable from food intended for normal human consumption, is suitable for its claimed particular nutritional purpose (*see* 2.28), and is sold in such a way as to indicate that suitability.

2.18 **Infants** means children under the age of twelve months.

2.19 **Ingredient** means any substance, including any additive and any constituent of a compound ingredient, which is used in the preparation of a food and which is still present in the finished product, even if in altered form, a compound ingredient being composed of two or more such substances.

2.20 **Intense sweetener** means an additive with a sweetness many times that of sucrose, which is virtually non-calorific and used solely for its sweetening properties.

2.21 **Labelling**, in relation to a food, includes any words, particulars, trade mark, brand name, pictorial matter or symbol relating to the food and appearing on the packaging of the food or on any document, notice, label, ring or collar accompanying the food.

2.22 **Milk** means the milk intended for sale, or sold, for human consumption of one or more cows (and includes skimmed milk, semi-skimmed milk and whole milk) or one or more ewes, goats or buffaloes.

2.23 **Mono-unsaturates** means fatty acids with one <u>cis</u> double-bond.

2.24 **Nutrient**, in the context of nutrition labelling, means any of the following: protein, carbohydrate, fat, fibre, sodium, any vitamin or mineral listed under 18.2 and present in any food in a significant amount as described under 21.4.

2.25 **Nutrition claim** means any statement, suggestion or implication in any labelling, presentation or advertising of a food that that food has particular nutrition properties, but does not include a reference to any quality or quantity of any nutrient where such reference is required by law.

2.26 **Nutrition labelling**, in relation to a food (other than a natural mineral water or other water intended for human consumption or any food supplement) means any information appearing on labelling (other than where such appears solely as part of a list of ingredients) and relating to energy value or any nutrient or to energy value and any nutrient, including any information relating to any substance which belongs to, or is a component of, a nutrient.

2.27 **Nutrition properties** means either or both of:

(a)   the provision (including provision at a reduced or increased rate), or the lack of provision, of energy;

(b)   the content (including content in a reduced or increased proportion), or the lack of content, of any nutrient (including any substance which belongs to, or is a component of, a nutrient).

2.28 **Particular nutritional purpose** means the fulfilment of the particular nutritional requirements of:

(a)   a person whose digestive processes are, or whose metabolism is, disturbed; or

(b)   a person whose physiological condition renders him able to obtain a special benefit from the controlled consumption of any substance in food; or

(c)   infants or young children in good health.

2.29 **Polyols** means the sweeteners: sorbitol and sorbitol syrup, mannitol, isomalt, maltitol and maltitol syrup, lactitol and xylitol.

2.30 **Polyunsaturates** means fatty acids with cis, cis-methylene interrupted double bonds.

2.31 **Prepacked**, in relation to a food, means put into packaging before being offered for sale in such a way that the food, whether wholly or only partly enclosed, cannot be altered without opening or changing the packaging and is ready for sale to the ultimate consumer (*see* 2.45) or to a catering establishment (*see* 2.4), and includes a food which is wholly enclosed in packaging before being offered for sale and which is intended to be cooked without opening the packaging and which is ready for sale to the ultimate consumer or to a catering establishment, but does not include individually wrapped sweets or chocolates which are not enclosed in any further packaging and which are not intended for sale as individual items.

2.32 **Prepacked for direct sale**, means:

(a)   in relation to a food other than flour confectionery, bread, edible ices and cows' milk, prepacked by a retailer for sale by him on the premises where the food is packed or from a vehicle or stall used by him;

(b)   in relation to flour confectionery, bread and edible ices, prepacked by a retailer for sale as in (a) or prepacked by the producer of the food for sale by him either on the premises where the food is produced or on other premises from which he conducts business under the same name as the business conducted on the premises where the food is produced; and

(c)   in relation to cows' milk, put into containers on the premises where the milk is produced by the person owning or having control of the herd from which the milk is produced for sale by him on those premises or from a vehicle or stall used by him.

2.33 **Preparation**, in relation to food, includes manufacture and any form of processing or treatment, and **prepared** should be construed accordingly.

2.34 **Processing aid** means any substance not consumed as a food by itself, intentionally used in the processing of raw materials, foods or their ingredients, to fulfil a certain technological purpose during treatment or processing, and which may result in the unintentional but technically unavoidable presence of residues of the substance or its derivatives in the final product, provided that these residues do not present any health risk and do not have any technological effect on the finished product.

2.35 **Process flavouring** means a product which is obtained according to good manufacturing practices by heating to a temperature not exceeding 180°C for a continuous period not exceeding 15 minutes a mixture of ingredients (whether or not with flavouring properties) of which at least one contains nitrogen (amino) and another is a reducing sugar.

2.36 **Protein** means the protein content calculated using the formula: protein = total Kjeldahl nitrogen $\times$ 6.25.

2.37 **Recommended daily allowance**, in relation to a vitamin or mineral, means the recommended daily allowance specified for that vitamin or mineral under 18.2.

2.38 **Saturates** means fatty acids without double bond.

2.39 **Seasonal selection pack** means a pack consisting of two or more different items of food which are wholly or partly enclosed in outer packaging decorated with seasonal designs.

2.40 **Sell** includes offer or expose for sale and have in possession for sale, and **sale** and **sold** should be construed accordingly.

2.41 **Smoke flavouring** means an extract from smoke of a type normally used in food smoking processes.

2.42 **Sterilised cream** means cream which has been subjected to a process of sterilisation by heat treatment in the container in which it is to be supplied to the consumer.

2.43 **Sugars**, in the context of nutrition labelling, means all monosaccharides and disaccharides present in food, but excludes polyols (*see* 2.29).

2.44 **Treating**, in relation to disease, includes doing or providing anything for alleviating the effects of the disease, whether it is done or provided by way of cure or not.

2.45 **Ultimate consumer** means any person who buys otherwise than for the purpose of resale, for the purposes of a catering establishment, or for the purposes of a manufacturing business.

2.46 **Young children** means children aged between one and three years.

CHAPTER 3

General labelling rules

3.1 Scope of general labelling rules

The general labelling rules outlined in this and the following chapters (3–15) apply to food which is ready for delivery to the ultimate consumer (*see* 2.45) or to a catering establishment (*see* 2.4).

These rules do not apply to a number of foods, including sugar products, cocoa products, chocolate products and honey, the labelling of which is governed by specific regulations. Nor do they apply to certain other foods, in so far as their labelling is governed by EC legislation.

Exemptions to some or all of these rules are extended to various foods (*see* 13).

3.2 General labelling rules

All foods, with the exception of those mentioned in 3.1, must be labelled with:

- a name (*see* 4);

- an ingredients list (*see* 5);

- the quantity of certain ingredients (*see* 10);

- a date mark (*see* 12);

- any special storage conditions or conditions of use (*see* 12.2);

- the name or business name and an address or registered office of the manufacturer or packer, or of a seller established within the EC;

- the place of origin, if failure to give it would be likely to mislead a purchaser as to the true origin of the food;

- instructions for use, if it would be difficult to make appropriate use of the food in the absence of such instructions. (Advice on appropriate instructions for raw minced beef, minced beef products, beefburgers, and raw flash-fried poultry products is given in Appendix 6.)

Note that in addition to these general labelling rules, further labelling particulars may be required, as follows:

- a quantity indication (*see* 17);

- a lot mark (*see* 16);

- an indication of the presence of packaging gas (*see* 14.6);

- an indication of the presence of sweeteners (*see* 14.5);

- a declaration of meat/fish/fruit and sugar content (*see* 14.7, 14.8 and 14.9).

CHAPTER 4

Name of the food

4.1   Name prescribed by law

Where there is a name prescribed by law, this must be used. Any such name may be qualified by other words which make it more precise. Names prescribed by law for species of fish, melons, potatoes and vitamins are listed in Appendix 1.

4.2   Customary name

If there is no name prescribed by law, a customary name, that is a name which is customary in the area where the food is sold, may be used. 'Eccles cake', 'Cornish pasty' and 'minestrone soup' are a few examples of the many customary names in use.

4.3   Descriptive name

If there is no name prescribed by law and no customary name, or the customary name is not used, a descriptive name must be used, that is a name which is sufficiently precise to indicate the true nature of the food and to enable it to be distinguished from products with which it could be confused. If necessary, the name should include a description of use. *See* 10.1 for examples of descriptive names.

4.4   Form of name

The name may consist of a name, a description or both.

4.5   Trade marks, brand names and fancy names

A trade mark, brand name or fancy name may not take the place of the name of the food, but may be used in addition to it.

4.6   Indication of physical condition or treatment

The name of a food must include, or be accompanied by an indication of its physical condition or treatment where a purchaser could be misled by the omission of that information. This could apply where a product is powdered or where it has been dried, freeze-dried, frozen, concentrated, smoked or subjected to any other treatment.

In particular, the name used for any meat which has been treated with proteolytic enzymes must include or be accompanied by the word 'tenderised', while the name used for a food which has been irradiated must include or be accompanied by the word 'irradiated' or the words 'treated with ionising radiation'.

Fish products incorporating minced fish (e.g. breaded scampi, fish fingers) may need to carry an appropriate indication on the label in cases where the consumer is likely to be misled, either on account of the general appearance of the food itself or its labelling, by the omission of such an indication.

It is important to ensure that an accurate indication of the process or treatment is given. Terms like roasted, smoked and filleted can be misleading where traditional processes have not been followed. For example, consumers may not necessarily associate roasting with a process involving a high proportion of steam cooking followed by a short period of flash roasting followed by the application of colour to simulate traditional roasting. The description 'roasted' should, however, be appropriate where a product has been roasted for sufficient time at a sufficient temperature to have the appearance, colour and texture of a roasted product.

A product which has simply been immersed in, or sprayed with, a solution which imparts flavour and colour has not been smoked, although it may be smoke flavoured.

Fish which has been de-boned and frozen into blocks before being sliced may need to be distinguished from fish which has been filleted in the traditional manner.

The name of cheeses made from raw milk should include an indication of this (*see* Appendix 6).

CHAPTER 5

List of ingredients

5.1   Heading of list of ingredients

The ingredients list must be headed or preceded by the word 'ingredients'. Additional words may be included, e.g. 'list of ingredients'.

5.2   Order of list of ingredients

Ingredients must be listed in descending order by weight, determined at the time of preparation of the food, i.e. normally at the 'mixing bowl' stage (but *see* 5.3).

5.3   Water and volatile ingredients

Water and volatile ingredients, such as alcoholic drinks added as such, must be listed in order of their weight in the finished product. Added water should be calculated by deducting from the total weight of the finished product the total weight of the other ingredients. Only when the added water exceeds 5% by weight of the finished product need it be declared. Water used solely for the reconstitution of a dried or concentrated ingredient need not be declared, nor need water used as a medium that is not normally consumed.

Water added to frozen or quick-frozen chicken carcasses in accordance with EC regulations need not be declared.

5.4   Reconstituted ingredients

It is permitted to list dried or concentrated ingredients, which are reconstituted during the preparation of the food, according to weight after reconstitution.

5.5   Mixed fruit, nuts, etc.

Where a food consists of, or contains, mixed fruit, nuts, vegetables, spices or herbs and no ingredient predominates significantly by weight, these ingredients may be listed otherwise than in descending order by weight, provided the ingredients list is accompanied by the words 'in variable proportion' or other appropriate words.

CHAPTER 6

Names of ingredients

6.1   Appropriate name

The name used for an ingredient should be a name which, if the ingredient itself were being sold as a food, could be used as the name of the food. Therefore, it should include an appropriate reference to physical condition or treatment (see 4.6), but only where omission of this information would mislead.

6.2   Irradiated ingredients

The name of an ingredient which has been irradiated must include or be accompanied by the word 'irradiated' or the words 'treated with ionising radiation'.

6.3   Generic names

Certain generic names, such as vegetable oil, cheese, sugar and fish, may be used instead of more specific names, as set out in Appendix 2.

6.4   Flavourings

Flavourings (*see* 2.13) may be described as 'flavouring' or 'flavourings', as appropriate, or given a more specific name, e.g. 'vanilla'.

The description 'natural flavouring' may be used only for flavouring preparations (*see* 2.14) and flavouring substances corresponding to the definition given in 2.15(a).

6.5   Declaration of additives

Additives belonging to the categories listed below must be identified by the category name followed by a specific name or serial number, if any (*see* Appendix 3). If an additive serves more than one function in the food concerned, it should be assigned to the category representing the principal function served. *See* Appendix 4 for criteria to be followed in selecting an appropriate specific name or serial number. An additive, which is neither a flavouring nor belongs to one of the categories below, must be identified by its specific name.

Additives which must be identified by category name

Acid[1]	Flour treatment agent
Acidity regulator	Gelling agent
Anti-caking agent	Glazing agent
Anti-foaming agent	Humectant
Antioxidant	Modified starch[2]
Bulking agent	Preservative
Colour	Propellant gas
Emulsifier	Raising agent
Emulsifying salt	Stabiliser
Firming agent	Sweetener
Flavour enhancer	Thickener

---

1   If the specific name of the acid includes the word 'acid', it is not necessary to use the category name.

2   Neither the specific name nor the serial number need be indicated. In the case of a modified starch which may contain gluten, the category name must be accompanied by an indication of the specific vegetable origin of the starch.

CHAPTER 7

Compound ingredients

7.1 Declaration of compound ingredients

Compound ingredients are those containing two or more ingredients. The names of the ingredients of a compound ingredient must be listed either instead of or in addition to the name of the compound ingredient itself (but *see* 7.2 for exemptions to this rule).

If the name of a compound ingredient is given, the names of its ingredients must follow it immediately in such a way as to make it clear that they are ingredients of that compound ingredient.

7.2 When ingredients of a compound ingredient need not be declared

The names of the ingredients of a compound ingredient need not to be given where:

(a) the compound ingredient would not be required to bear a list of ingredients if it were itself being sold prepacked; or

(b) the compound ingredient is identified by a generic name as described in 6.3; or

(c) the compound ingredient constitutes less than 25% of the finished product and any declarable additives (*see* 6.5 and 8) present in the compound ingredient are named immediately after the name of the compound ingredient.

CHAPTER 8

Ingredients which need not be named

The following ingredients need not be named in an ingredients list:

(a)   Constituents of an ingredient which have become temporarily separated during the manufacturing process and are later re-introduced in their original proportions (e.g. the yolk and white of an egg separated during manufacture need not be listed separately, but may be declared as 'egg' in the ingredients list);

(b)   Any additive whose presence in the food is due solely to the fact that it was contained in an ingredient of the food, if it serves no significant technological function in the final product (e.g. antioxidant present in a bread fat to extend its shelf life need not not be declared in the bread, as it no longer serves any significant function there);

(c)   Any additive which is used solely as a processing aid (e.g. calcium sulphate added to bread dough as a yeast nutrient need not be declared, as it is used as a processing aid);

(d)   Any substance other than water which is used as a solvent or carrier for an additive and is used in an amount that is no more than that which is strictly necessary for that purpose.

CHAPTER 9

Foods which need not bear a list of ingredients

9.1 Exempted foods

The following foods need not be labelled with an ingredients list:

(a)   fresh fruit and vegetables, including potatoes, which have not been peeled or cut into pieces;

(b)   carbonated water, to which no ingredient other than carbon dioxide has been added, and whose name indicates that it has been carbonated;

(c)   vinegar which is derived by fermentation exclusively from a single basic product and to which no other ingredient has been added;

(d)   cheese, butter, fermented milk and fermented cream, to which no ingredient has been added other than lactic products, enzymes and micro-organism cultures essential to manufacture or, in the case of cheese other than fresh curd cheese and processed cheese, such amount of salt as is needed for its manufacture;

(e)   flour to which no substances have been added other than the statutory nutrients;

(f)   any drink with an alcoholic strength by volume of more than 1.2%;

(g)   any food consisting of a single ingredient, where the name of the food is identical to the name of the ingredient or enables the nature of the ingredient to be clearly identified.

In the case of (c) and (d) above where other ingredients have been added, only these other added ingredients need be declared in the ingredients list, provided the list is headed by the words 'added ingredients' or similar.

9.2   If a list of ingredients is given

If a food that is not required to bear a list of ingredients is labelled with an ingredients list then that list must be a complete list in accordance with the rules applying to foods that do have to bear a list of ingredients.

CHAPTER 10

Indication of quantities of certain ingredients

This section concerns quantitative ingredient declaration, otherwise known as QUID. Note that QUID becomes compulsory for food prepacked after 14 February 2000. Food prepacked before this date may instead be labelled in accordance with the special emphasis provisions set out in 11.

10.1 When QUID is necessary

Apart from certain exemptions (see 10.2), the quantity of an ingredient or category of ingredients used in the preparation of a food must be indicated where that ingredient or category of ingredients:

(a)   appears in the name of the food or is usually associated with that name by the consumer;

(b)   is emphasised on the labelling in words, pictures or graphics; or

(c)   is essential to characterise a food and to distinguish it from products with which it might be confused because of its name or appearance.

Guidance on the interpretation of these rules is given below.

A QUID declaration does not apply:

•   to constituents naturally present in foods, which have not been added as ingredients, such as caffeine in coffee or vitamin C in fruit juices; or

- to ingredients which, although mentioned in the name of the food, have not been used in its preparation. Examples are 'cream crackers' (cream not present) and 'smokey bacon flavoured crisps' (the flavour derives from ingredients other than bacon).

QUID does apply where:

- The ingredient is included in the name of the food. Examples: 'ham and mushroom pizza', 'strawberry yogurt', 'steak and kidney pie', 'salmon mousse', 'pork sausage'. In these examples, the underlined ingredients must be quantified;

- The category of ingredient is included in the name of the food. Examples: 'vegetable pasty', 'fish cakes', 'nut loaf', 'fruit pie'. Here, only the total vegetable, fish, nut and fruit, respectively, need be quantified;

- An ingredient or category of ingredient is usually associated with the name of the food by the consumer (*see* Table 10.1).

Table 10.1

Product example	Example of descriptive name	QUID for:
Lancashire hotpot	Mutton and potatoes with onions, carrots and gravy	Mutton
Chilli con carne	Minced beef with kidney beans, tomatoes, peppers, onion and chilli	Minced beef
Fisherman's pie	Cod and haddock with peas in a white sauce, topped with mashed potato	Fish
Summer pudding	Strawberries, raspberries, blackberries, redcurrants and blackcurrants set in a light gel with bread	Fruit
Spring rolls	Bean sprouts, peas and carrots in a light crispy pancake	Vegetables

- The ingredient or category of ingredients is emphasised on the labelling in words, pictures or graphics. Examples: use of flashes, such as 'with extra chicken', 'made with butter', or 'with real cream'; use of a different size, colour and/or style of lettering to refer to particular ingredients anywhere on the label other than in the name of the food; use of pictorial representation to emphasise selectively one or more ingredients, for example fish casserole with a prominent picture or illustration of only a selection of the fish ingredients.

•   The ingredient or category of ingredients is essential to characterise a food and to distinguish it from products with which it might be confused because of its name or appearance. This provision is intended to cover those products, the composition of which can differ markedly from one member state to another, but which are usually marketed under the same name. The only examples agreed at EU level are mayonnaise and marzipan.

QUID is unlikely to be required for such products made in the UK for the UK market, but may be required for those made in the UK for sale in other member states.

10.2   Exemptions from QUID

Exemptions from QUID apply to an ingredient or category of ingredients:

(a)   the drained net weight as well as the net weight of which is declared on the label;

(b)   the quantities of which are already required to be declared under EC law;

(c)   which is used in small quantities for the purposes of flavouring;

(d)   which, though it appears in the name of the food, is not such as to govern the choice of the consumer because the variation in quantity is not essential to characterise the food or does not distinguish it from similar foods;

(e)   the quantity of which is regulated by EC law without requiring it to be declared on the label.

(f)   QUID also does not apply where a food consists of, or contains, mixed fruit, nuts, vegetables, spices or herbs and no ingredient predominates significantly by weight (*see* 5.5).

Guidance on how these exemptions apply is given below.

Any food presented in a liquid medium which declares the **drained net weight** and the net weight on its label is exempt from the need to give a separate QUID declaration, because this can be calculated from the weight indications already given. Examples include: a single type of vegetable in water; a single type of fruit in juice; sardines in brine; and frozen prawns. The exemption does not apply if, on mixed ingredient products, one or more is emphasised in some way, because the amount of the emphasised ingredient cannot be calculated from the weight indications already given.

The exemption for ingredients used for **flavouring** is not limited to flavourings that are additives, but applies also to any ingredient or category of ingredients which has been used in a small quantity to flavour a food, for example garlic, herbs or spices. 'Small quantity' is taken to mean a level of 2% or less by weight, calculated from the recipe at the 'mixing bowl' stage, excluding carriers and diluents. Examples of products covered by this exemption are: 'Dry London Gin' with a picture of juniper berries on the label; 'Lemonade/Orangeade' and other similar soft drinks where the flavour comes wholly or mainly from use of flavourings which are additives; 'cinnamon Danish', 'herb dumpling', 'garlic bread' and other products which refer to herbs, spices or other ingredients with a strong flavour (either specifically or generically) in their name, or which are usually associated by consumers with the use of such herbs, spices or other ingredients.

QUID rules do not apply to an **ingredient mentioned in the name of a food, the quantity of which is not essential to characterise the food or distinguish it from similar foods.** In such cases the quantity of the ingredient will not affect a consumer's purchasing decisions. This exemption presupposes that the presence of the ingredient is not emphasised on the label. The following products are thought to be covered by this exemption:

- alcoholic drinks, such as malt whisky/whiskey;

- liqueurs and fruit based spirits which mention an ingredient in their name;

- rye bread and other breads (including rolls and flour confectionery), which mention a cereal or seed ingredient in their name;

- products which mention several minor ingredients in their name, for example 'chicken platter, including potatoes, peas and carrots' (where the exemption will apply to the vegetable ingredients);

- dried pasta which mentions the use of more than one type of wheat on its label;

- products, such as processed cheese and tomato ketchup, in which consistency depends on the recipe rather than the quantity of the named ingredient;

- products, such as pickles and sauces, which are highly processed and in which it is only the spices and/or flavourings which are likely to distinguish one product from another;

- products, such as snacks, which are essentially mixtures of carbohydrate, oil/fat and flavourings.

A QUID declaration is not necessary for mixtures of, for example, fruit, vegetables, spices or herbs, where the ingredients are present in more or less equal proportions by weight.

10.3 Form of QUID

The quantity of ingredient declared should generally be calculated by weight from the recipe at the 'mixing bowl' stage, not including in the calculation any water or volatile ingredients lost during processing. The quantity of volatile ingredients such as alcohol, however, should relate to that present by weight in the finished product.

It should be a typical quantity, rounded to the nearest whole number, reflecting the producer's normal manufacturing variations in accordance with good manufacturing practice.

QUID declarations should relate to the ingredient as identified in the ingredients list. Ingredients identified, for example, as 'chicken', 'milk', 'egg' or 'banana' should be quantified as raw/whole, as the names used imply use of the basic food because they carry no indication that they have been processed. Ingredients identified by names which indicate they have been used other than in their raw/whole form, e.g. 'roast chicken', 'skimmed milk', 'crystallised fruit', should be quantified as used. Declarations of processed ingredients may be supplemented with 'raw equivalent' declarations, since this would help consumers compare similar products which have used ingredients in different forms.

QUID declarations on concentrated or dehydrated products intended to be reconstituted before consumption (including dry mixes for cakes and desserts) should relate to the ingredients in the reconstituted product if the ingredient listing information is also given on this basis. In deciding whether to give ingredient listing and QUID information based on either the dehydrated or reconstituted product, consideration should be given to avoiding giving QUID and any nutrition labelling information on different bases on the same label.

The quantity declaration must appear in or next to the name of the food or in the ingredients list. It need appear only once on the label, as convenient. Alternatively, the indication may appear in a separate line associated with the ingredients list in those cases where the category of ingredients referred to in the name of the food is not used as such in the ingredients list or where a 'raw equivalent' declaration is given (*see* above). Products exempt from ingredient listing must give the indication in or next to the name of the food.

CHAPTER 11

Ingredients given special emphasis

Note that the provisions outlined in this section apply only to foods prepacked before 14 February 2000 and as an alternative to QUID (*see* 10).

11.1 Declaration of minimum content

Where a food is characterised by the presence of a particular ingredient, the labelling of the food must not place special emphasis on the presence of that ingredient unless it includes a declaration of the minimum percentage of that ingredient in the food, determined as at the time of its use in the preparation of the food.

11.2 Declaration of maximum content

A similar provision applies to foods characterised by the low content of particular ingredients. In such cases the declaration of the maximum content of the relevant ingredient in the food must be made.

11.3 Form of declaration

The appropriate declaration must appear next to the name of the food or in the ingredients list close to the name of the ingredient in question.

11.4   Flavourings in small quantities

A reference to an ingredient which is used in a small quantity and only as a flavouring does not of itself constitute the placing of special emphasis on the presence or low content of that ingredient.

11.5   Criteria for special emphasis

A reference in the name of a food to a particular ingredient does not necessarily constitute the placing of special emphasis, but this could depend on the size, colour and/or style of lettering used. Particulars, including the name of the food, which have to be given on the label by law are not of themselves regarded as giving special emphasis. Where the presence, or absence, of a particular ingredient is prominently stated more than once on a label, other than in a restatement of the name of the food, this may be deemed to be special emphasis.

CHAPTER 12

Date mark

12.1 Types of date mark

There are two types of date mark, as below.

(a)   The words 'best before' followed by the date up to and including which the food can reasonably be expected to retain its specific properties, if properly stored. This form of date mark is appropriate for most foods.

(b)   The words 'use by' followed by the date up to and including which the food, if properly stored, is recommended for use. A 'use by' date must be used for foods which are highly perishable from a microbiological point of view and are therefore likely after a short period to constitute an immediate danger to human health.

See Appendix 5 for guidance on what foods should carry a 'use by' date.

12.2 Storage conditions

The 'best before' date and the 'use by' date must be followed by any storage conditions which need to be observed, such as 'keep refrigerated' or 'keep in a cool, dry place'.

12.3   Form of date mark

The date must be expressed as a day, month and year in that order. Alternatively:

- for foods expected to keep for 3 months or less – the date may be given as a day and month;

- for foods expected to keep for 3 months, but no longer than 18 months – the date mark may be shown as 'best before end' followed by the month and year (not applicable to 'use by' dates);

- for foods expected to keep for more than 18 months – the date mark may be shown as 'best before end' followed by the month and year or the year only (not applicable to 'use by' dates).

12.4   Signposting

The date, or the date and any necessary storage conditions, may appear on the labelling separately from the words 'best before', 'best before end' or 'use by', provided that those words are followed by a reference to the place where the date or the date and storage conditions appear. This might be indicated on the front of the pack, for example, by the words 'for best before date, see side of pack and for storage conditions, see star marking panel' or by the words 'for best before date, see side of pack', while declaring on the side of the pack the date and the words 'for storage conditions, see star marking panel'.

12.5   Exemptions

The following foods need not carry a date mark:

- fresh fruit and vegetables (including potatoes but not including sprouting seeds, legume sprouts and similar products) which have not been peeled or cut into pieces;

- wine, liqueur wine, sparkling wine, aromatised wine and any similar drink obtained from fruit other than grapes;

- any drink made from grapes or grape musts and coming within codes 2206 00 39, 2206 00 59 and 2206 00 89 of the Combined Nomenclature given in Council Regulations (EEC) No. 2658/87 on the tariff and statistical nomenclature and on the Common Customs Tariff, as amended;

- any drink with an alcoholic strength by volume of 10 per cent or more;

- any soft drink, fruit juice or fruit nectar or alcoholic drink, sold in a container containing more than 5 litres and intended for supply to catering establishments;

- any flour confectionery and bread which, given the nature of its content, is normally consumed within 24 hours of its preparation;

- vinegar;

- cooking and table salt;

- solid sugar and products consisting almost solely of flavoured or coloured sugars;

- chewing gums and similar products;

- edible ices in individual portions.

12.6 Offences

It is an offence to sell a food beyond its 'use by' date. It is also an offence to alter or remove a date mark if you are not the manufacturer, packer or EC seller originally responsible for marking the food. It is, however, a defence for anyone so charged to prove that such action was taken with the written authorisation of a person capable of making the change without breaking the law.

CHAPTER 13

Exemptions from some or all of the labelling rules

13.1 Exemptions from labelling

The following are exempted from the general labelling rules (*see* 3.2):

(a)   non-prepacked food;

(b)   food prepacked for direct sale (*see* 2.32);

(c)   flour confectionery (*see* 2.16) packed in a crimp case only or in wholly transparent packaging which is either unmarked or marked only with the price and/or lot mark (*see* 16);

(d)   individually wrapped fancy confectionery products (*see* 2.11) which are not enclosed in any further packaging and are intended for sale as single items.

All such food, however, except for white bread, flour confectionery, food which is not exposed for sale, and carcasses and parts of carcasses which are not intended for sale in one piece, must be marked with a name. Where appropriate, milk must be marked with its place of origin (*see* 3.2) and, if such milk is raw (i.e. untreated), with the name and address of the manufacturer or packer.

Separate rules apply to food sold at catering establishments (*see* 13.5).

13.2   Indication of additives

A food which is exempted by 13.1 from ingredients listing, but contains the following additives which would otherwise have to be declared (*see* 8), must be labelled with an indication of their presence: antioxidant, colour, flavouring, flavour enhancer, preservative, sweetener.

In the case of edible ices (*see* 2.10) or flour confectionery (*see* 2.16) covered by this exemption, it is sufficient to display a notice in a prominent position near the products concerned stating that they may contain these additives (note that only the category of additive need be declared). This requirement relates only to the principal function served by an additive.

13.3   Irradiated ingredients

Where an exempted food contains an ingredient that has been irradiated, the presence of that ingredient must be declared and described as 'irradiated' or 'treated with ionising radiation'.

13.4   Small packages and certain glass bottles

Foods contained in small packages (the largest surface of the packaging having an area of less than $10cm^2$) or in indelibly marked glass bottles intended for re-use and having no label, ring or collar, need be labelled only with a name and, where appropriate, a date mark. Such bottles containing milk must be marked with its place of origin where appropriate (*see* 3.2) and, if such milk is raw (i.e. untreated), with the name and address of the manufacturer or packer. Such bottles containing milk need not be labelled with a date mark.

A prepacked food sold or supplied as an individual portion, and intended as a minor accompaniment to either another food or another service (e.g. food supplied in a hotel room) need be labelled only with a name. This includes individual portions of butter and other fat spreads, milk, cream and cheeses, jams and marmalades, mustards, sauces, tea, coffee and sugar.

13.5   Certain food sold at catering establishments

Any food sold at a catering establishment (*see* 2.4) which is either not prepacked or prepacked for direct sale (*see* 2.32) is exempt from labelling, unless it has been irradiated, in which case it must be labelled with the declaration 'irradiated' or 'treated with ionising radiation'. If the food contains an ingredient that has been irradiated, the name of that ingredient must be given accompanied by a similar declaration. Milk prepacked for direct sale (*see* 2.32) must be marked with its place of origin where appropriate (*see* 3.2) and, if such milk is raw (i.e. untreated), with the name and address of the manufacturer or packer.

13.6   Seasonal selection packs

The outer packaging of a seasonal selection pack (*see* 2.39) need not be labelled, provided that each item contained in the pack is individually prepacked and appropriately labelled.

CHAPTER 14

Additional labelling for certain foods

14.1 Food sold from vending machines

The name of a food sold from a vending machine must appear on a notice on the front of the machine, unless the name appears on the labelling of the food in such a manner as to be easily visible and clearly legible to an intending purchaser through the outside of the machine.

Where such food is not prepacked and the subject of a nutrition claim (*see* 2.25), nutrition labelling (*see* 21) must appear on a notice either on the front of the machine or in close proximity to the machine in such a way as to be readily discernible by an intending purchaser.

Where such food should be reheated properly before it is eaten, but suitable instructions for reheating are not given on the packaging (if any), they must be given on a notice as described in the previous paragraph.

14.2 Prepacked alcoholic drinks

Prepacked alcoholic drinks, other than Community controlled wine, with an alcoholic strength by volume of more than 1.2% must be labelled with that alcoholic strength in the form of a figure to not more than one decimal place (which may be preceded by the word 'alcohol' or by the abbreviation 'alc') followed by the symbol '%vol'.

Positive and negative tolerances permitted in respect of alcoholic strength by volume, expressed in absolute values, are as below.

Alcoholic drink	Positive or negative tolerance
1. (a) Beers having an alcoholic strength not exceeding 5.5% volume;	
(b) alcoholic drinks made from grapes and falling within subheading No. 2206–0093 and No. 2206–0099 of the combined nomenclature (1988).	0.5% vol.
2. (a) Beers having an alcoholic strength exceeding 5.5% volume;	
(b) alcoholic drinks made from grapes and falling within subheading No. 2200–0091 of the combined nomenclature (1988);	
(c) ciders, perries, fruit wines and other wines obtained from fruits other than grapes whether or not semi-sparkling or sparkling;	1% vol.
(d) alcoholic drinks based on fermented honey.	
3. Alcoholic drinks containing macerated fruit or parts of plants.	1.5% vol.
4. Any other alcoholic drink.	0.3% vol.

Note: The above tolerances apply without prejudice to the tolerances deriving from the method of analysis used for determining the alcoholic strength.

For the purposes of this regulation, the alcoholic strength of any drink must be determined at 20°C.

14.3   Raw milk

The container in which raw milk is sold must be labelled with the words 'This milk has not been heat-treated and may therefore contain organisms harmful to health'.

Raw milk sold non-prepacked at a catering establishment (*see* 2.4) must be labelled with the words 'Milk supplied in this establishment has not been heat-treated and may therefore contain organisms harmful to health', which must appear either on a label attached to the container or on a ticket or notice that is readily discernible by an intending purchaser when choosing the milk.

These provisions do not apply to raw milk from buffaloes.

14.4   Milk substitutes

The container of a milk substitute consisting of skimmed milk with non-milk fat and which is not specially formulated for infants or young children must be labelled with a warning that the product is unfit, or not to be used, as food for babies.

14.5   Food containing sweeteners

A food containing a sweetener or sweeteners must be labelled with the indication 'with sweetener(s)', which must accompany the name of the food.

A food containing both an added sugar or sugars and a sweetener or sweeteners must be labelled with the indication 'with sugar(s) and sweetener(s)' which must accompany the name of the food.

A food containing aspartame must be labelled with the indication 'contains a source of phenylalanine'.

A food containing more than 10% added polyols (*see* 2.29) must be labelled with the indication 'excessive consumption may produce laxative effects'.

14.6   Modified atmosphere packs

A food which has been packaged in a packaging gas for the purpose of extending its shelf life must be labelled with the indication 'packaged in a protective atmosphere'. If the packaging gas has been used for some other technological purpose, there is no need to include the declaration on the label unless it also serves to extend the shelf life of the food.

The declaration is not compulsory in the following circumstances:

*   where the gas is used at the packaging stage to solve a technical problem inherent in such packaging; e.g. in the brewing industry, where bottling would be impossible for pressure reasons without the use of gases at the packaging stage; e.g. in the packaging of soft drinks in aluminium cans in order to prevent deforming the packaging; e.g. instant coffee, which has a very high moisture content, where the gas is used to avoid the agglomeration of the product;

- where the gas is naturally present in the food, even if operations such as extraction followed by reincorporation are needed at the packaging stage; e.g. when packaging coffee beans or ground coffee;

- where the gas is added in order to give the food its particular organoleptic characteristics; e.g. to carbonated water and soft drinks, in which case the gas will be declared in the ingredients list.

The declaration does not apply to foods which have been vacuum packed.

14.7   Declaration of meat content

Meat products must be labelled with a declaration of meat content in the form 'minimum X% meat'. For those with a meat content of less than 10% or more than 100%, the declarations 'less than 10% meat' or 'not less than 100% meat', respectively may alternatively be used. The word 'meat' may be replaced by the name of the type of meat.

Where a product is required to be labelled with an ingredients list, the declaration must appear in immediate proximity to it. Where only one type of meat is present, it is sufficient for the declaration to appear in the list next to the name of the ingredient concerned, in which case the word 'meat' or name of the type of meat may be omitted.

For non-prepacked products or those prepacked for direct sale, the required declaration may appear on a ticket or notice displayed beside them or on an attached label. *See* note in 14.8.

14.8   Declaration of fish content

Spreadable fish products (fish paste, fish pâté, fish spread, etc.) must be labelled with a declaration of fish content in the form 'minimum Y% fish'. For those with a fish content of more than 100% the declaration 'not less than 100% fish' may alternatively be used. The word 'fish' may be replaced by the name of the type of fish. The manner in which this declaration should be made is as in 14.7.

Note that a declaration of meat/fish content may be omitted if a quantitative ingredient declaration has been given on the label in accordance with 10.3.

14.9   Declaration of fruit and sugar content of jam

The fruit content of jam and similar products must be declared in the form 'prepared with Xg of fruit per 100g', where X represents the quantity in g of fruit (i.e. fruit pulp, fruit purée, fruit peel and aqueous extract of fruit) used for every 100g of finished product.

The sugar content of these products must be declared using the words 'total sugar content: Yg per 100g' where Y denotes the soluble solids content determined by refractometer at 20°C, accurate to ±3 refractometric degrees. Products specially made for diabetics and labelled as such are exempt from this requirement.

Declaration of fruit and sugar contents is not required for fruit curd, fruit flavour curd, mincemeat, products for immediate consumption or products sold to a manufacturer for the purposes of his business.

These particulars must appear on the label in the same field of vision as the name, the quantity mark and the date mark.

In the case of reduced sugar jam, reduced sugar jelly, reduced sugar marmalade and UK standard jelly, a declaration of the fruit and sugar contents may be omitted if a quantitative ingredient declaration has been given on the label in accordance with 10.3.

CHAPTER 15

Manner of labelling

15.1 General requirement

In general, labelling information prescribed for prepacked foods must appear on:

- the packaging, or

- a label attached to the packaging, or

- a label that is clearly visible through the packaging.

However, where a prepacked food is sold otherwise than to the ultimate consumer (*see* 2.45), this information may appear, alternatively, in relevant commercial documents furnished on or before delivery of the food, provided that the name, date mark and name and address of the manufacturer, packer or seller also appears on the outermost packaging in which the food is sold.

15.2 Certain exempted foods

When food to which 13.1 or 13.5 applies is sold to the ultimate consumer (*see* 2.45), the prescribed labelling information must appear on:

- a label attached to the food, or

- a menu, notice, ticket or label that is readily discernible by an intending purchaser when choosing the food.

Where there is no label attached to the food and it contains an ingredient that has been irradiated, it is sufficient to declare on a menu, notice, ticket or label, that the food may contain that irradiated ingredient, using the description 'irradiated' or 'treated with ionising irradiation'.

A similar provision relates to the use in a catering establishment (*see* 2.4) for seasoning of herbs and spices that have been irradiated.

When food to which 13.1 applies is sold otherwise than to the ultimate consumer (*see* 2.45), the prescribed labelling information must appear on:

- a label attached to the food, or

- a ticket or notice that is readily discernible by the intending purchaser when choosing the food, or

- in relevant commercial documents furnished on or before delivery of the food.

15.3   Bottled milk

For bottled milk, the prescribed labelling information may be given on the bottle cap. For bottled raw milk, however, the declaration mentioned in 14.3 must be given elsewhere than on the bottle cap.

15.4   Intelligibilty

There are no requirements as to the size and type of letters to be used in labelling (apart from quantity marking, *see* 17), but labelling particulars must be easy to understand, clearly legible and indelible and, when a food is sold to the ultimate consumer (*see* 2.45), they must be marked in a conspicuous place in such a way as to be easily visible. Individually, they must not be hidden, obscured or interrupted by any other written or pictorial matter. For example, the name of the food must not be broken up by other material, nor must the ingredients list, but it is acceptable for the ingredients list itself to be shown separately from the name of the food.

These rules do not preclude information being given at a catering establishment (*see* 2.4) in respect of foods, the variety and type of which are changed regularly, by means of temporary media (including the use of chalk on a blackboard).

15.5 Field of vision

The following information, where prescribed, must appear at least once in the same field of vision:

• the name

• the date mark

• an indication of alcoholic strength by volume

• the cautionary words in respect of raw milk

• the warning mentioned in 14.4

• the quantity mark.

The date mark, alcoholic strength and weight mark need not appear in the same field of vision in the case of the foods referred to in 13.4.

CHAPTER 16

Lot mark

16.1   Purpose and form of lot mark

The Food (Lot Marking) Regulations 1996 require most foods (*see* 16.3 and 16.4 for exemptions) to carry a mark identifying the lot (or batch) of which they formed part. This is to facilitate product recall in the event of an emergency, such as a health risk to consumers.

The lot mark must appear on the label or prepacked foods and, where it is not clearly distinguishable from other information on the label, it must be prefixed by the letter 'L'.

16.2   Size of a lot

It is for the manufacturer, packer or seller to determine the size of a lot.

16.3   Exemptions

The following foods do not require a lot mark:

*   individual items of food which at point of sale to the ultimate consumer (*see* 2.45) are not prepacked, such as loose sweets, fruit and vegetables;

- foods prepacked for direct sale (*see* 2.32) or prepacked at the request of the purchaser;

- individual goods not intended to be sold separately, such as single tea bags or chocolates;

- foods in a package or container, the largest side of which has a surface area of less than 10cm^2;

- individual portions intended as an accompaniment to another food provided at a catering establishment (*see* 2.4) for immediate consumption, such as sachets of salt, sauce or sugar. Also excluded are tea bags, coffee etc. provided as part of another service, for example, drink making facilities in hotel rooms; and

- individual portions of ice cream and other edible ices (*see* 2.10).

16.4   Use of date mark as lot mark

A date mark may be used as a lot mark, including in cases where the product is not required to carry a date mark, provided that the date mark is given in accordance with the rules (*see* 12).

Note that using a date mark as a lot mark could result in the size of a lot being unacceptably large, incurring the risk of withdrawal of, for example, a batch of at least one month's production.

CHAPTER 17

Quantity mark

17.1 Exemptions

Weights and measures legislation requires most prepacked foods to carry an indication of quantity by net weight or by volume. Prepacked foods which are exempt from quantity marking include the following:

- foods (except saffron) in a quantity of less than 5g or 5ml;

- biscuits, prepacked on the premises where baked and weighing 100g or less;

- biscuits (other than wafer biscuits which are not cream-filled) weighing 50g or less;

- bread weighing less than 300g;

- bun loaves, fruit loaves, malt loaves and fruited malt loaves;

- chocolate products weighing less than 50g;

- fancy chocolate products (*see* 2.11), provided the net weight (when not less than 50g) is given on a ticket or notice displayed on the products or in immediate proximity to them;

- cocoa products weighing less than 50g;

- fish pies;

- flour confectionery (*see* 2.16) except when consisting of or including uncooked pastry or shortbread;

- freeze drinks in a quantity of less than 50ml;

- herbs, whole and sifted except saffron, in a quantity of less than 25g;

- iced lollies and water ices;

- meat pies, meat puddings and sausage rolls;

- potato crisps and other snack foods in a quantity of less than 25g;

- poultry pies;

- shortbread, in a quantity not exceeding 50g, or consisting of a piece or pieces each weighing 200g or more if the number of pieces in the container, if more than one, is marked on the container or is clearly visible and capable of being easily counted through the container;

- single toffee apples;

- sugar confectionery consisting of rock or barley sugar in sticks or novelty shapes;

- sugar confectionery and chocolate confectionery in a quantity of less than 50g.

17.2 Marking by number

Certain prepacked foods, containing more than one item, are required to be marked by number, including the following:

- cereal biscuit breakfast foods, except when none of the biscuits weighs more than 10g;

- flour confectionery (*see* 2.16), except when consisting of uncooked pastry or uncooked pastry cases, not containing any filling, or shortbread and except where the number of items in the container is clearly visible and capable of being easily counted through the container;

- fruit preservative tablets, rennet tablets, saccharin tablets, soft drink tablets and sweetening tablets;

- shell eggs;

- vanilla pods;

- capsule and tablet foods.

17.3   Metric or imperial units

Quantity marks must be in metric units but may, in addition, be in imperial units. In such cases, the metric units must be indicated first. Where the marking is in both metric and imperial units, these indications must be of equal size and be distinct but in close proximity to each other and nothing may be inserted between them.

17.4   Permitted units and declarations

The units commonly used and permitted for quantity marking of foods, together with the permitted symbols or abbreviations, are listed below. The letter 's' may be added to an abbreviation, when appropriate, but not to a symbol.

Metric unit	Symbol	Imperial unit	Abbreviation
litre	l (or L)	gallon	gal
centilitre	cl	quart	qt
millilitre	ml	pint	pt
kilogram	kg	fluid ounce	fl oz
gram	g	pound	lb
		ounce	oz

Apart from certain exemptions applying to catchweight products, i.e. any food product which because of its nature is not prepacked according to a pre-determined fixed weight pattern, but is prepacked in varying quantities, the following rules apply to the marking of food containers.

Quantity marking. A quantity mark required by law must consist of the numerical value of the relevant unit expressed in words or figures and a reference to that unit either by words or a permitted symbol or abbreviation (*see* above). Where the numerical value of the unit is expressed in words, the unit or measurement must be expressed in words and not by means of a symbol or abbreviation.

A **metric** quantity must not be expressed as a vulgar fraction. '**Net**' or '**gross**' may not be abbreviated.

17.5   Field of vision

A quantity mark must appear on the label in the same field of vision as the name (*see* 15.5). It is subject to the same requirements as to legibility, etc. (*see* 15.4) as apply generally to labelling information.

17.6   Minimum size

Unlike other labelling information, quantity marks are subject to minimum size requirements. The figures forming part of a quantity mark must be at least the height specified below.

Mass or weight of contents	Min height of figures (mm)
Not more than 50g	2
More than 50g but not more than 200g	3
More than 200g but not more than 1kg	4
More than 1kg	6

The numerator and denominator together indicating a vulgar fraction must appear one on top of the other and for the purposes of the minimum height requirement indicated above are to be treated as a single figure.

17.7 'E' mark

Prepacked foods made up in accordance with the average system may carry the 'e' mark, which must be at least 3mm high. Use of the 'e' mark facilitates the export of packaged goods within the EU. Where a packer intends to export packages bearing an 'e' mark, he must give written notice to his local weights and measures authority before the end of the day on which the packages are made up.

CHAPTER 18

Nutrition claims 1

18.1 Prohibited claims

The following types of claim may not be made, either expressly or by implication, in any labelling or advertising.

1.   A claim that a food has tonic properties (use of the description 'Indian tonic water' or 'quinine tonic water' does not constitute such a claim).

2.   A claim that a food has the property of preventing, treating or curing a human disease or any reference to such a property. (Claims relating to foods for particular nutritional uses, referred to below, are not regarded as being in this category.)

18.2 Restricted claims

The following types of claim may only be made, either expressly or by implication, in the labelling or advertising of a food, when the conditions indicated in each case are satisfied.

Foods for particular nutritional uses (*see* 2.17)

To claim that a food is suitable, or has been specially made, for a particular nutritional purpose (*see* 2.28):

1.   The food must be capable of fulfilling the claim.

2.   The food must be labelled with the particular aspects of its composition or manufacturing process that give it its particular nutritional characteristics.

3.   The food must be labelled with nutrition information (*see* 21) which may include any nutrient or component of a nutrient, whether or not it is the subject of a claim, or any other component or characteristic which is essential to the food's suitability for its particular nutritional use.

4.   The food, when sold to the ultimate consumer (*see* 2.45), must be prepacked and completely enclosed by its packaging.

Reduced or low energy value claims

To claim that a food has a **reduced energy value**, the energy value of a given weight of the food, or a given volume in the case of a liquid food, must not be more than three quarters of that of the equivalent weight, or volume, of a similar food in relation to which no such claim is made, unless the food is an intense sweetener, or a product which consists of a mixture of an intense sweetener with other substances and which, when compared on a weight for weight basis, is significantly sweeter than sucrose.

To claim that a food has a **low energy value**:

1.   The energy value of the food must not be more than 167kJ (40kcal) per 100g or 100ml, as is appropriate, unless the food is an intense sweetener, or a product which consists of a mixture of an intense sweetener with other substances and which, when compared on a weight for weight basis, is significantly sweeter than sucrose.

2.   The energy value of a normal serving of the food must not be more than 167kJ (40kcal).

3.   In the case of an uncooked food which naturally has a low energy value, the claim must be in the form 'a low energy food' or 'a low calorie food' or 'a low Joule food'.

Nutrition information (*see* 21) is required for both **reduced and low energy value claims.**

Notes

1.   The appearance, on the container of a soft drink, of the words 'low calorie' (*see* 22.1) does not of itself constitute a **reduced or low energy value claim.**

2.   Where a food is in concentrated or dehydrated form and is intended to be reconstituted by the addition of water or other substances, the conditions applying to **low energy value claims** should relate to the food when reconstituted as directed.

Protein claims

To claim that a food is a source of protein, the quantity of the food that can reasonably be expected to be consumed in one day must contribute at least 12g of protein. In addition, if the claim is that the food is a rich or excellent source of protein, at least 20% of the energy value of the food must be provided by protein. In any other case, at least 12% of the energy value of the food must be provided by protein. The food must be labelled with nutrition information (*see* 21).

Note that these conditions do not apply to foods intended for babies or young children which satisfy the conditions applying to foods for particular nutritional uses (*see* above).

Vitamin claims

To claim that a food is a source of vitamins:

1.   Every vitamin named in the claim must be a vitamin specified in the table below. If the claim is

that the food is a rich or excellent source of vitamins, the quantity of the food that can reasonably be expected to be consumed in one day must contain at least one half of the recommended daily allowance (RDA) (*see* table) of every vitamin named in the claim or, where the claim is not confined to named vitamins, of two or more of the vitamins specified in the table. In the case of other claims, the corresponding proportion of the RDA must be at least one sixth.

2. The food must be labelled with nutrition information (*see* 21) to include those vitamins, whether or not named, which are the subject of the claim. The information must also include the % RDAs of these vitamins contained in either a quantified serving or, provided the number of portions contained in the pack is stated, in a portion of the food. The names used for vitamins must be those appearing in the table below.

Note that a reference to a vitamin in the name of a vitamin mixture or a vitamin and mineral mixture does not itself constitute a claim.

Mineral claims

The conditions to be satisfied are identical to those for vitamins.

Vitamins in respect of which claims may be made	
Vitamin	**Recommended daily allowance (RDA)**
Vitamin A	800µg
Vitamin D	5µg
Vitamin E	10mg
Vitamin C	60mg
Thiamin	1.4mg
Riboflavin	1.6mg
Niacin	18mg

Vitamin B$_6$	2mg
Folacin/Folic acid	200µg
Vitamin B$_{12}$	1µg
Biotin	0.15mg
Pantothenic acid	6mg

Minerals in respect of which claims may be made

Mineral	Recommended daily allowance
Calcium	800mg
Phosphorus	800mg
Iron	14mg
Magnesium	300mg
Zinc	15mg
Iodine	150µg

Cholesterol claims

To justify a claim relating to the presence or absence of cholesterol in a food:

1. It must contain no more than 0.005% of cholesterol.

2. The suggestion, whether express or implied, that the food is beneficial to human health because of its level of cholesterol, must not be made.

3. If the claim relates to the removal of cholesterol from, or its reduction in, the food and condition 1 is not met, the claim may only be made –

    (a) as part of an indication of the true nature of the food,

(b) as part of an indication of the treatment of the food,

(c) within the list of ingredients, or

(d) as a footnote in respect of nutrition information.

4.   The food must be labelled with nutrition information (*see* 21).

Nutrition claims

Any nutrition claim not dealt with above must satisfy the following conditions:

1.   The food must be capable of fulfilling the claim.

2.   The food must be marked or labelled with nutrition information (*see* 21).

Claims which depend on another food

A claim that a food has a particular value or confers a particular benefit may be made only when the value or benefit is not derived wholly or partly from another food that is intended to be consumed with the food concerned.

18.3   Supplementary provisions relating to claims

The conditions with which claims must comply are not intended to prevent the dissemination of useful information or recommendations intended exclusively for persons having qualifications in dentistry, medicine, nutrition, dietetics or pharmacy.

A reference to a substance in a list of ingredients or in any nutrition information (*see* 21) does not of itself constitute a claim of the type described in 18.2.

Non-prepacked foods sold in catering establishments, and which are the subject of a claim, including one contained within generic advertising, need not be labelled with nutrition information (*see* 21), although it may be given. When given, amounts per 100g may be supplemented by amounts in an unquantified serving or in any one portion of the food.

CHAPTER 19

Nutrition claims 2

19.1 Scope of claims

'Guidelines for the use of certain nutrition claims in food labelling and advertising' have been issued by MAFF. They provide advice on the criteria to be used in relation to certain popular nutrition claims and are based on recommendations made by the Food Advisory Committee in 1989. The guidelines are advisory and have no legal effect. Nevertheless, it would be prudent to comply with them when making any of the claims to which they apply.

The claims relate to the following nutrients: fat (*see* 2.12), saturates (*see* 2.38), sugar(s) (*see* 2.43), salt/sodium and fibre.

The types of claim covered are: low, no added, free/without, source, increased, reduced, more/less and high/rich.

19.2 Criteria for claims

As for all nutrition claims, nutrition information (*see* 21) must be given when making one of these claims and it must include the nutrient which is the subject of the claim.

The criteria for making these claims are given below.

Low. Claims that a food is low in fat, saturates, sugar(s) or salt/sodium should conform to the conditions in Table 19.1. Claims for foods naturally low in a nutrient should take the form 'a low x food'.

No added. Claims that a food contains no added sugars or salt should conform to the conditions in Table 19.1.

X free/without. Claims that a food is free from or without fat, saturates, sugar(s) or salt/sodium should conform to the conditions in Table 19.1.

Source. A claim that a food is a source of fibre should conform to the conditions in Table 19.1.

Increased. A claim that a food has an increased fibre content should conform to the conditions in Table 19.1. Increased claims for other nutrients should only be made when there is a minimum 25% increase of the nutrient contained in the food compared with the normal product, i.e. the standard version of the product, for which no claim is made.

Reduced. Claims that a food has a reduced content of a nutrient should only be made when there is a minimum 25% reduction of the nutrient contained in the food compared with the normal product, i.e. the standard version of the product, for which no claim is made. *Notes:* use of the term 'reduced sugar' for jams and similar products which comply with the *Jam and Similar Products Regulations 1981* and the *Jam and Similar Products (Scotland) Regulations 1981* is not considered to be a claim of this type; separate criteria apply to the use of the term 'reduced fat' when referring to spreadable fats.

More/less. Claims that a food contains less than 25% more or less of a nutrient should take the form 'contains Y% more/less X'.

High/rich. Claims that a food has a high fibre content or is rich in fibre should conform to the conditions in Table 19.1. Claims for foods naturally high in fibre should take the form 'a high fibre food'.

For **concentrated** or **dehydrated** food which is intended to be reconstituted by the addition of water or any other substance, the claims conditions apply to the food after it has been reconstituted as directed.

Table 19.1 Conditions for making claims

	Low	No added	X free
Fat	No more than 5g in either a normal serving of food for which this is more than 100g or 100ml *or* in 100g or 100ml of a food for which the normal serving is less than this amount.[1] In the case of a food naturally low in fat the claim must be made in the form 'a low fat food'.		No more than 0.15g per 100g or 100ml.
Saturates	No more than 3g in either a normal serving of a food for which this is more than 100g or 100ml *or* in 100g or 100ml of a food for which the normal serving is less than this amount. In the case of a food naturally low in saturates the claim must be made in the form 'a low saturates food'.		No more than 0.1g per 100g or 100ml.
Sugar(s)	No more than 5g in either a normal serving of a food for which this is more than 100g or 100ml *or* in 100g or 100ml of a food for which the normal serving is less than this amount. In the case of a food naturally low in sugars the claim must be made in the form 'a low sugar(s) food'.	No sugars or foods composed mainly of sugars added to the food or to any of its ingredients.[2]	No more than 0.2g per 100g or 100ml.
Salt/ Sodium	No more than 40mg in either a normal serving of a food for which this is more than 100g or 100ml *or* in 100g or 100ml of a food for which the normal serving is less than this amount.	No salts of sodium shall have been added to the food or to any of its ingredients.	No more than 5mg per 100g or 100ml.

In the case of a food naturally low in salt/sodium the claim must be made in the form ' a low salt/ sodium food'.

	Source	**Increased**	**Rich**
Fibre	Either 3g per 100g or 100ml *or* at least 3g in the reasonably expected daily intake of the food. In the case of a food naturally high in fibre, the claim must take the form 'a high fibre food'.	At least 25% more than a similar food for which no claim is made *and* at least 3g in either the reasonably expected daily intake of a food for which this is higher than 100g or 100ml *or* in 100g or 100ml.	Either at least 6g per 100g or 100ml *or* at least 6g of the reasonably expected daily intake of the food.

1. The description 'low fat' when applied to spreadable fats and the description 'low fat soft cheese' in accordance with the *Cheese Regulations 1970* are not considered to be claims of this type.

2. This claim includes use of the term 'unsweetened' except in accordance with the provisions of the *Condensed Milk and Dried Milk Regulations 1977*.

CHAPTER 20

Use of the word 'natural' and similar terms

MAFF has issued recommended conditions for the use of the term 'natural' in food labelling and advertising with the intention that they should be observed on a voluntary basis by the food industry. They are based on Food Advisory Committee guidelines and are set out below.

20.1   When 'natural' may be used

The term 'natural' without qualification should be used only in the following cases.

(a)   To describe single foods, of a traditional nature, to which nothing has been added and which have been subjected only to such processing as to render them suitable for human consumption.

- Freezing, concentration, fermentation, pasteurisation, sterilisation, smoking (without chemicals) and traditional cooking processes such as baking, roasting or blanching are examples of processes which would be acceptable.

- Bleaching, oxidation, smoking (with chemicals), tenderising (with chemicals) and hydrogenation and similar processes clearly fall outside.

- As a general rule for single ingredient foods such as cheese, yoghurt and butter, acceptable processing is that which is strictly necessary to produce the final product.

– The restriction to 'foods of a traditional nature' is intended to exclude novel foods, which may technically be products of natural sources but which do not accord with the public perception of 'natural'.

(b) To describe food ingredients obtained from recognised food sources and which meet the criteria in (a).

(c) To describe permitted food additives obtained from recognised food sources by appropriate physical processing (including distillation and solvent extraction) or traditional food preparation processes.

(d) To describe flavourings when in conformity with the UK *Flavourings in Food Regulations* and EC Directives 91/71/EEC and 91/72/EEC.

(e) To describe preserved tuna and bonito when in conformity with EC Regulation 1536/92.

20.2 Compound foods

Compound foods should not therefore be described directly or by implication as 'natural', but it is acceptable to describe such foods as 'made from natural ingredients' if *all* the ingredients meet the criteria in 20.1(b) or (c).

20.3 'Natural' taste flavour or colour

A food which does not meet the criteria in 20.1(a) or 20.2 should not be claimed to have a 'natural' taste, flavour or colour.

20.4 Brand or fancy names

'Natural', or its derivatives, should not be included in brand or fancy names nor in coined or meaningless phrases in such a way as to imply that a food which does not meet the criteria in 20.1(a) is natural or made from natural ingredients.

20.5   Meaningless claims

Claims such as 'natural goodness', 'naturally better', or 'nature's way' are largely meaningless and should not be used.

20.6   'Natural' meaning plain or unflavoured

'Natural' meaning no more than plain or unflavoured should not be used except where the food in question meets the criteria at 20.1(a) or 20.2.

20.7   'Real', 'genuine', 'pure', etc.

The principles set out above also apply when other words similar to 'natural', such as 'real', 'genuine', 'pure' which have separate and distinctive meanings of their own, are used in place of 'natural' in such a way as to imply similar benefits to consumers.

20.8   Negative claims

Other claims (which might be termed 'negative claims') which do not use the term 'natural' or its derivatives, but the effect of which is to imply 'naturalness' to the consumer are potentially misleading and confusing. At least the following should not be used:

1.   a claim that a food is 'free from X' if all foods in the same class or category are free from 'X';

2.   statements or implications which give undue emphasis to the fact that a product is free from certain non-natural additives, when the product contains other non-natural additives;

3.   a claim that a food is 'free from' one category of additive when an additive of another category, or an ingredient, having broadly similar effect is used.

The conditions do not affect 'negative claims' which do not imply 'naturalness' to the consumer, (such as 'free from X', where 'X' is a particular additive), and which may provide them with accurate and beneficial information.

CHAPTER 21

Nutrition information

21.1 General

The provision of nutrition information on food labels is purely voluntary, unless a nutrition claim (*see* 2.25) is made or the food is one for a particular nutritional use (*see* 2.17), when it becomes compulsory. However, when nutrition information is given, whether on a voluntary or compulsory basis, it must comply with the rules below. These rules do not apply to food supplements or to natural mineral waters and other waters for human consumption.

21.2 Prescribed formats

When nutrition information is provided, a Group 1 or Group 2 format must be used as set out below. A nutrient for which a claim has been made must be included.

Group 1 (also known as the 'big 4')	
Energy	kJ and kcal
Protein	g
Carbohydrate	g
Fat	g

Group 2 (also known as the 'big 4 + little 4' and '4 +4')	
Energy	kJ and kcal
Protein	g
Carbohydrate	g
of which:	
– Sugars	g
Fat	g
of which:	
– Saturates	g
Fibre	g
Sodium	g

21.3   Other nutrients which may be declared

The following nutrients may be added to a Group 1 or Group 2 declaration on a voluntary basis, but must be declared if a claim about them is made:

polyols as a breakdown of carbohydrate

starch as a breakdown of carbohydrate

mono-unsaturates* as a breakdown of fat

polyunsaturates* as a breakdown of fat

cholesterol* as a breakdown of fat

vitamins**

minerals**

*   when one of these is declared, saturates **must** also be declared.

**   only listed vitamins and minerals (*see* 18.2) may be declared, and they must be present in significant amounts (*see* 21.4).

Any nutrient not listed above may only be declared if a claim has been made about it and it is a component of a nutrient as defined (*see* 2.24).

'As a breakdown of' means, for example, in the case of polyols that declaration should take the form:

Carbohydrate	g
of which	
– polyols	g

21.4 Vitamins and minerals

Vitamins and minerals which may be included in a nutrition declaration are listed under 18.2. They may be included only if present in a significant amount, which as a rule means that at least 15% of the RDA should be supplied by 100g of the food or, for packages containing a single portion, by a package of the food.

Vitamins should be declared before minerals in the order shown and using the names listed under 18.2. It should be acceptable to give a more familiar name in brackets, e.g. 'thiamin (vitamin B_1)'.

Vitamins should be calculated according to the following table:

Vitamin	To be calculated as
Vitamin A	retinol *or* retinol equivalent to the basis that 6µg of ß-carotene or 12 µg of other biologically active carotenoids equal 1µg of retinol equivalent.
Vitamin D	ergocalciferol (vitamin D_2) *or* cholecalciferol (vitamin D_3)
Vitamin E	D-α tocopherol equivalent on the basis that 3.3mg α tocotrienol or 10mg γ tocopherol are equivalent to 1mg D-α tocopherol
Vitamin C	l-ascorbic acid and l-dehydroascorbic acid
Thiamin	thiamin
Riboflavin	riboflavin

Niacin	nicotinic acid *or* nicotinamide *or* niacin equivalent on the basis that 60mg of tryptophan equal 1mg of niacin equivalent
Vitamin B_6	pyridoxine
Folacin/Folic acid	total folates
Vitamin B_{12}	cobalamines
Biotin	biotin
Pantothenic acid	D-pantothenic acid

21.5 Supplementary requirements

Amounts of energy and nutrient per 100g or 100ml of the food must be given, although amounts per quantified serving or, provided the total number of portions in the pack is stated, per portion of the food may also be given, if desired.

A portion is either a division of a package as a whole, e.g. half a quiche, a sausage, a sixth of a cake, two biscuits, or a complete package. A quantified serving is a measured amount, which may or may not be a division of a whole package, such as Xg of cheese or Yml of mayonnaise.

Amounts given must relate to the food as ready for sale, except that where sufficiently detailed instructions for preparation are given, they may relate to the food as ready for consumption, provided that this is made clear on the label.

Average values must be declared based, either alone or in any combination, on:

• the manufacturer's analysis; or

• calculation from known average values of the ingredients; or

• calculation from generally-established and accepted data.

Average values means those which best represent the amounts of nutrients present, taking into account seasonal variability, patterns of consumption and any other factor which may cause the actual amount to vary.

Nutrition information must be presented together in one conspicuous place in tabular form with any numbers aligned or, where there is insufficient space for tabular listing, in linear form. A combination of tabular and linear listing is not acceptable.

When a nutrient is present in a quantity of less than 0.1g per 100g/100ml, declarations of '0g', 'trace', 'nil' or 'negligible' are thought to be acceptable. Figures of between 0.05g and 0.15g, however, can be rounded to 0.1g and that value used instead.

In cases where it is difficult to analyse for a nutrient and it is found to be present in an amount equal to the limit of detection, e.g. 0.2g per 100g, it should be acceptable to declare 'less than 0.2g'.

21.6 Definition of fibre

Fibre (sometimes referred to as dietary fibre) has still not been defined either at UK or EC level. MAFF continues to advise that, for the purposes of nutrition labelling, it should be defined as non-starch polysaccharides, as determined by the Englyst method and having a dietary reference value of 18g per day (as recommended by COMA, the Committee on Medical Aspects of Food and Nutrition Policy). Nevertheless, analysts may use other methods which give similar results, the AOAC (Association of Official Analytical Chemists) method being that most frequently used in the UK and throughout the EU for the determination of fibre to be declared on food labels.

21.7 Energy conversion factors

The following conversion factors (per gram) must be used in the calculation of the energy value:

	kJ	kcal
Carbohydrate (excluding polyols)	17	4
Polyols	10	2.4
Protein	17	4
Fat	37	9
Ethanol	29	7
Organic acid	13	3

An energy conversion factor is not prescribed for polydextrose, but MAFF has agreed with LACOTS that a factor of 5kJ/1kcal may be used.

21.8   Non-prepacked foods

If a claim is made about a non-prepacked food, nutrition information need be given only for the nutrient that is the subject of the claim, although information may be given voluntarily for any or all energy, Group 2 nutrients, permitted vitamins or minerals.

21.9   Foods sold by caterers

Non-prepacked food sold at a catering establishment (*see* 2.4) need not carry nutrition information even if a claim is made, although information may be given per 100g or per portion.

21.10 PARNUT foods

Foods for particular nutritional uses are required to carry information on their special nutrient properties, even when this would not be permitted on normal food (*see* 18.2). For instance, the gluten content must be declared on a food suitable for coeliacs, even though no specific gluten claim has been made. Likewise, declarations of fructose and/or individual polyols may be given on a food for diabetics, because these contribute to the PARNUT properties of the food.

Claims that a food is suitable for diabetics are not prohibited. However, specially formulated 'diabetic foods' are considered unnecessary in the dietary management of diabetes. Current dietary advice to diabetics from health professionals is that management of diabetes is best achieved through consumption of a normal well-balanced diet. A food carrying a claim that it is suitable for, or has been specially made for diabetics must be capable of fulfilling the claim and be labelled with an indication of what makes it suitable for diabetics (*see* 18.2).

21.11 Food supplements

Food supplements are exempt from the rules on nutrition information. If a claim in respect of vitamins and/or minerals is made on a food supplement, the percentage RDA per portion and an indication of the number of portions contained in the pack must be given.

21.12 Waters

Natural mineral waters and other waters for human consumption are exempt from the rules on nutrition information.

CHAPTER 22

Misleading descriptions

22.1 Use of certain descriptions

The following conditions apply to the use of certain descriptions for food.

Dietary or dietetic

These descriptions may not be used unless the food has been specially made for a class of persons whose digestive process or metabolism is disturbed, or who obtain special benefit from a controlled consumption of certain substances, and the food is suitable for fulfilling the particular nutritional requirements of that class of persons.

Flavours

Descriptions which include the name of a food in such a way as to imply that the product, or the part of the product being described has the flavour of the food concerned must not be used unless the flavour of the product is derived wholly or mainly from the flavouring food. In the case of a description including the word 'chocolate' such as to imply that the product being described has a chocolate flavour, this must be derived wholly or mainly from non-fat cocoa solids. If these conditions are not fulfilled, for example if the flavour of the product derives mainly from synthetic flavouring, the expression 'X flavour' may be used, as appropriate.

Pictorial representations

When these are used so as to imply that a food has the flavour of the ingredient depicted, the flavour of the food must be derived wholly or mainly from that ingredient.

Ice cream

This description may be applied only to the frozen product containing not less than 5% fat and not less than 2.5% milk protein, not necessarily in natural proportions, and which is obtained by subjecting an emulsion of fat, milk solids and sugar (including any sweetener permitted in ice cream), with or without the addition of other substances, to heat treatment and either to subsequent freezing or evaporation, addition of water and subsequent freezing.

Dairy ice cream

This description may be applied only to a product conforming to the description 'ice cream' given above, provided the minimum 5% fat is exclusively milk fat and that the product contains no fat other than milk fat, apart from fat present in any egg, flavouring, emulsifier or stabiliser used as an ingredient of the ice cream.

Milk

The word 'milk' must not be used as part of the name of a food which contains the milk of an animal other than a cow unless:

• it is accompanied by the name of that animal; and

• the milk has all its normal constituents in their natural proportions *or* it has been subjected to a process or treatment, e.g. skimming, and an indication of that process or treatment is given.

The word 'milk' must not be used as the name of an ingredient consisting of the milk of an animal other than a cow unless it is accompanied by the name of that animal.

Starch-reduced

This description must not be used unless less than 50% of the food consists of anhydrous carbohydrate, on a dry basis, and the starch content of the food is substantially less than that of similar foods to which the description is not applied.

Vitamin

This word, or any other word or description implying the same, may be used only to describe one of the vitamins listed in 18.2 or vitamin K.

Alcohol-free

This description may not be applied to any alcoholic drink from which the alcohol has been extracted, unless it has an alcoholic strength by volume of not more than 0.05% and it is labelled with its maximum alcoholic strength as in 14.2 or, where appropriate, with an indication that it contains no alcohol.

Dealcoholised

Similar conditions attach to the use of this description as to the previous item, except that the alcoholic strength by volume must be not more than 0.5%.

Low alcohol

This description or any other indication implying the same must not be applied to any alcoholic drink unless it has an alcoholic strength by volume of not more than 1.2% and it is marked with its maximum alcoholic strength as in 14.2.

Low calorie

This description or any other indication implying the same must not be applied to any soft drink unless it contains not more than 10 kcal/42kJ per 100ml (after dilution or other preparation, where applicable).

Non-alcoholic

This description may be used only in the composite name 'non-alcoholic wine' to describe a drink derived from unfermented grape juice which is intended exclusively for communion or sacramental use and is labelled as such.

Liqueur

This description may be applied only to a drink complying with the definition of liqueur given in EC regulations.

Indian tonic water or Quinine tonic water

These names may be used only for drinks containing not less than 57mg of quinine (calculated as quinine sulphate B.P.) per litre.

Tonic wine

This name may be used to describe a drink only if there appears in immediate proximity the clear statement 'the name 'tonic wine' does not imply health-giving or medicinal properties' and no recommendation as to consumption or dosage is given.

Wine

This name may be used in a composite name for a drink which is not wine as defined in EC regulations, but only if it is unlikely to cause confusion with wine or table wine as defined and the composite name appears in lettering of the same type and colour and of such a height that it is clearly distinguishable from other particulars.

When the word 'wine' is used in a composite name for a drink which is derived from fruit other than grapes, that drink must be obtained by an alcoholic fermentation of that fruit.

22.2   Names for cheese

The following names may not be used for cheese unless:

(a)   the amount of water, expressed on the total weight of the cheese, does not exceed that specified below; and

(b)   the amount of milk fat in the cheese, expressed on the dry matter, is not less than 48%.

Variety of cheese	Maximum percentage of water
Cheddar	39
Blue Stilton	42
Derby	42

Leicester	42
Cheshire	44
Dunlop	44
Gloucester	44
Double Gloucester	44
Caerphilly	46
Wensleydale	46
White Stilton	46
Lancashire	48

22.3   Names for cream

The following names may not be used for cream, unless it complies with the corresponding conditions, as set out below. The relevant requirement as to milk fat content need not be complied with if the name contains qualifying words which indicate that the milk fat content of the cream is greater or less than that specified. In calculating the percentage of milk fat in any cream, any ingredient added to the cream should be disregarded.

Name of cream	Conditions
Clotted cream	The cream is clotted and contains not less than 55% milk fat
Double cream	The cream contains not less than 48% milk fat
Whipping cream	The cream contains not less than 35% milk fat
Whipped cream	The cream contains not less than 35% milk fat and has been whipped
Sterilised cream	The cream is sterilised and contains not less than 23% milk fat
Cream or single cream	The cream is not sterilised cream and contains not less than 18% milk fat
Sterilised half cream	The cream is sterilised cream and contains not less than 12% milk fat
Half cream	The cream is not sterilised cream and contains not less than 12% milk fat

CHAPTER 23

Protection of dairy designations

23.1 Protected designations

Certain designations used in the marketing of milk and milk products are protected in law. The protected designations, apart from 'milk', are:

whey	buttermilk	anhydrous milkfat (AMF)	
cream	butteroil	cheese	kephir
butter	caseins	yoghurt	koumiss

These names may be qualified appropriately, e.g. Cheddar cheese, double cream. The origin of the milk or milk product must be stated, if it is not cow's milk.

The protected designations may not be used at any stage of marketing in labelling, advertising or presentation in such a way as to claim, imply or suggest that a product other than one of those listed above, is a dairy product. This applies to brand, fancy and trade names as well as to a name required in law.

23.2 Exemptions

Exemptions apply to:

1. composite products such as cheesecake or brandy butter, provided none of the dairy constituents have been replaced;

2.   descriptions of a characteristic quality of a product, e.g. creamed rice;

3.   products the exact nature of which is clear from traditional usage.

A list of traditional products, mentioned in 3 above, forms part of EC legislation and is reproduced below. The list is not thought to be comprehensive, so that any name containing a dairy reference which has traditionally been used should not be subject to restriction.

List of traditional products

Coconut milk

'Cream...' or 'Milk...' used in the description of a spirituous beverage not containing milk or other
    milk products or milk or milk product imitations (e.g. cream sherry, milk sherry)

Cream soda

Cream filled biscuits (e.g. custard cream, bourbon cream, raspberry cream biscuits, strawberry cream,
    etc.)

Cream filled sweets or chocolates (e.g. peppermint cream, raspberry cream, crème egg)

Cream crackers

Salad cream

Creamed coconut and other similar fruit, nut and vegetable products where the term 'creamed'
    describes the characteristic texture of the product

Cream of tartar

Cream or creamed soups (e.g. cream of tomato soup, cream of celery, cream of chicken, etc.)

Horseradish cream

Ice-cream

Jelly cream

Table cream

Cocoa butter

Shea butter

Nut butters (e.g. peanut butter)

Butter beans

Butter puffs

Fruit cheese (e.g. lemon cheese, damson cheese)

CHAPTER 24

Labelling of organic foods

The Organic Products Regulations currently cover only products of plant origin, although it is intended to extend them to include animal products also. In the meantime it should be acceptable to label animal products as 'organic' provided they comply with the rules applying to organic production, etc.

According to the regulations, the word 'organic' or similar may be used to describe only unprocessed agricultural crop products and processed products composed of one or more ingredients of plant origin. It should refer to organic production methods, e.g. 'organically grown carrots' or 'white bread made from organically produced wheat'.

Processed products may be described as 'organic' only where:

(a)   at least 95% of the ingredients of agricultural origin were produced organically;

(b)   the remaining 5% or less of ingredients of agricultural origin are not produced organically at all or in sufficient quantity in the EC or on import from third countries;

(c)   only approved ingredients of non-agricultural origin were used;

(d)   neither the product nor any of its ingredients were irradiated or processed using non-approved processing aids;

(e)   the product was prepared by a registered operator;

(f)   the label must refer to the name and/or a code number of the relevant inspection body.

The word 'organic' or similar may be used in the ingredients list of a processed product only where:

(a)   at least 70% of the ingredients of agricultural origin were produced organically;

(b)   the remaining 30% or less of ingredients of agricultural origin are not produced organically at all or in sufficient quantity in the EC or on import from third countries;

(c)   conditions (c), (d), (e) and (f) above are satisfied;

(d)   the ingredients and their relative levels appear in descending order by weight in the ingredients list;

(e)   the organic reference appears in lettering of the same colour, size and style as the other indications in the list of ingredients;

(f)   a separate statement must appear in the same field of vision as the product name in the form 'X% of the agricultural ingredients were produced in accordance with the rules of organic production'. The statement may not appear in a colour, size and style of lettering which is more prominent than the product name.

CHAPTER 25

Beef Labelling Scheme

The Beef Labelling Scheme which became operational from 1 January 1998 was set up by MAFF and implements EU regulations. It enables retailers to provide consumers with information, other than the basic particulars such as are required in law, about fresh and frozen beef and veal, and minced beef and veal, provided they have obtained prior approval. Other beef and veal products are not covered.

This voluntary scheme is in place in all EU countries until 31 December 1999. After that retailers will have to get approval for all their beef labels. They will also then have to tell consumers what country their beef comes from.

Examples of information for which approval is needed under the scheme are:

- the origin of the beef, i.e. where the animal was born, raised or slaughtered;

- breed (e.g. Galloway);

- age or sex;

- identification number of animal;

- method of production (e.g. organic, extensively-reared, grass-fed);

- method of slaughter (e.g. Halal, Kosher);

- date of slaughter;

- method or length of maturation.

It is necessary to be able to prove that this information is true, and to employ an independent third party to verify the system for ensuring this. The system must guarantee a link between the beef and the animal or animals from which it came, and this involves keeping comprehensive records.

A unique reference code or number and the company's name or logo must appear on the label together with the information being given to the consumer.

Retailers wishing to participate in the Scheme should obtain an application form from MAFF at the address below. MAFF is also able to provide further details of the Scheme and a list of organisations recognised for the purpose of verification.

Beef Labelling Section

Ministry of Agriculture, Fisheries and Food

Room 416, Whitehall Place (West Block)

London SW1A 2HH

Helpline: Tel: 0171 270 8958

　　　　　　 Fax: 0171 270 8836

CHAPTER 26

Labelling of genetically modified foods

26.1   GM foods considered as novel foods

Since 15 May 1997, genetically modified (GM) foods have been subject to EC Regulation No. 258/97 concerning novel foods and novel food ingredients. Novel foods are foods or food ingredients that have not been used for human consumption to a significant degree in the EU and/or have been produced by extensively modified or entirely new food production processes. Foods containing or derived from genetically modified organisms (GMOs) are considered as novel foods.

The Regulation requires novel foods to undergo a pre-market approval process and, for products which are not 'substantially equivalent' to existing foods or food ingredients, this will involve a full safety evaluation.

Special labelling is necessary if live GMOs are present or where there are particular ethical concerns, for example if human genes have been incorporated or if animal genes have been introduced into a plant food. The form that this labelling should take, however, has not yet been specified. It is permissible, however, to indicate that the food is not of GMO origin or that GMOs may be present, in particular in the case of bulk consignments.

Many GM foods do not fall within these categories and therefore there is no special labelling requirement, nor is there if the inserted gene has been destroyed during processing and, consequently, is not present in the final food.

26.2 Voluntary labelling and EC developments

In response to consumer demand, certain manufacturers and retailers have chosen to label all foods and food ingredients which are the product of gene technology so as to clearly indicate their origin regardless of whether or not this labelling is required in law. Such labelling is already mandatory in a number of other member states. In the UK, the FAC has consistently recommended that where labelling of GM foods is not compulsory, it should be given voluntarily in view of consumer interest.

Eventually all GM products will require specific labelling, as the European Commission has already issued a press release (July 1997) indicating its intention to bring this about and, thereby, to ensure a coherent EU approach. The type of labelling proposed would be:

- Voluntary labelling (e.g. 'this does not contain…') for certified non-GMO produce.

- Mandatory labelling (e.g. 'this contains…') for produce known to be of GMO origin. A possibility for operators to voluntarily indicate, in addition, the proportion of produce of GMO origin in mixed products could be envisaged.

- Mandatory labelling (e.g. 'this may contain…') in cases where material of GMO origin cannot be excluded but where no evidence of such material is available.

The 'may contain' label is not particularly helpful to consumers and would be limited by requiring that it is replaced by 'contains…' whenever there is either documentary/label evidence or testing has shown the presence of GMO material.

Specific product lists would be prepared so as to give guidance as to which products to label.

26.3   GM soya and GM maize

Ingredients derived from GM soya and GM maize, which have been arriving in the UK mostly from the USA, are not subject to the EC Novel Foods Regulation because they were already on the market before it became law. To rectify this anomaly, an EC regulation came into force on 1 November 1997 applying the same labelling requirements to GM soya and GM maize as those contained in the EC Novel Foods Regulation. It has now been superseded by Council Regulation (EC) No. 1139/98, which lays down detailed rules for the labelling of food ingredients obtained from GM soya and GM maize. These rules became compulsory in member states on 1 September 1998.

Where a GM ingredient has been used and, taking the example of soya flour as an illustration, one of the following declarations must be made in the ingredients list:

*   soya flour (produced from genetically modified soya); or

*   soya (genetically modified) flour; or

*   soya* flour

    Then as a footnote to the ingredients list and in lettering no smaller than the ingredient list:

    *   genetically modified; or

    *   produced from genetically modified soya.

Where there is no ingredients list, the words 'produced from genetically modified soya' must appear clearly on the product label. Where a generic name is used in the ingredients list (*see* 6.3), it must be followed by the words 'contains soya flour produced from genetically modified soya'. Where the soya flour is the ingredient of a compound ingredient, the words 'produced from genetically modified soya' must appear clearly on the product label.

Exactly the same labelling principles apply to GM maize ingredients.

These rules do not apply to products manufactured and labelled prior to 1 September 1998, nor to products in which neither protein nor DNA resulting from genetic modification is present. The

Regulation also grants a six month transition period for products where other forms of wording have been used to indicate the presence of GM material.

It is intended to prepare a list of products not subject to these labelling rules for the benefit of food manufacturers and retailers.

CHAPTER 27

Future developments

27.1 Future of the '25% rule'

Under the '25% rule', the names of the ingredients of a compound ingredient need not be declared, if the compound ingredient constitutes less than 25% of the final product, although any functional additives present must be named (*see* 7.2(c)).

There is a view that because of this provision the consumer does not receive sufficiently detailed information about the exact composition of the food he is purchasing. As a result it has been suggested that the '25% rule' should be removed altogether, while a proposal has been put to the Codex Committee on Food Labelling (an international expert organisation) that it should be amended to 5%.

Changes to this rule are imminent, at least as regards the declaration of allergens (*see* 27.2), if not concerning foods generally.

27.2 Labelling of allergens

Currently, there is no specific requirement to declare the presence of allergens on food labels. Many manufacturers and retailers have chosen voluntarily to assist those consumers who may have concerns in this matter by highlighting the presence of severe allergens, such as peanuts, where it might not be obvious or where it would not otherwise be required by law. Statements such as 'this product does not contain peanuts' have also proved helpful.

Where there is a possibility of cross-contamination during manufacture, it is appropriate to make the statement 'may contain nut traces' on products where nuts are not actually used as ingredients. It is important, however, not to use such a statement as a substitute for good manufacturing practice and manufacturers should take all reasonable steps to prevent cross-contamination of food. The FAC has suggested that where peanuts are not a characteristic ingredient of a product, manufacturers should consider whether peanuts and their derivatives could be replaced by alternative ingredients.

There is a draft proposal to amend the EC Labelling Directive to make it compulsory to include certain ingredients causing food intolerance or allergy in the list of ingredients. If accepted, this amendment would become law in member states. Those foods and ingredients recognised as causing hypersensitivity which would have to be declared are:

- cereals containing gluten and products of these
- crustaceans and products of these
- eggs and egg products
- fish and fish products
- peanuts and products of these
- soyabeans and products of these
- milk and milk products (lactose included)
- tree nuts and nut products
- sesame seeds
- sulphite at concentrations of at least 10mg/kg

Under this proposal the '25% rule' (*see* 27.1) would not apply to the above ingredients nor would the exemption from declaration of the ingredients of compound ingredients identified by a generic name (*see* 7.2(b)) or of those ingredients mentioned under 8(b), (c), and (d).

27.3   Compulsory nutrition information?

The UK government has submitted a number of suggestions to the European Commission as to how the Nutrition Labelling Directive might be amended, as it is currently under review. This directive governs the manner in which nutrition information is provided on food labels throughout the EC. As a forewarning of possible changes to this area of labelling, an abbreviated version of the UK submission is given below.

1.   Nutrition labelling should be compulsory whether or not a claim has been made

In order for consumers to benefit fully from the use of nutrition information and thereby improve their diet and enhance their health, it is important that nutrition labelling should appear on all labels, not just on those making claims. The UK considers the time is right for such a move since it is estimated that, in the UK at least, some 80% of prepacked foods already carry nutrition labelling. Making it compulsory would therefore not have a major effect on the majority of businesses.

2.   More information should be given in the prescribed format

Currently the minimum (Group 1) information required consists of the energy value and the amount of protein, carbohydrate and fat per 100g or 100ml of the food. In the interests of providing more detailed nutrition information for the benefit of the consumer, the UK considers this should be expanded to include saturates, sugars, sodium and fibre. If fuller nutrition labelling is made mandatory, the current exemption for ingredient listing on small packages should be extended to nutrition labelling.

3.   Compulsory per serving information

Consideration should be given to making compulsory per serving or per portion information in addition to per 100g/ml information or introducing some other more user-friendly format. Consumers find per serving information more meaningful and useful. Nevertheless, information per 100g is the easier means of comparing quantities of nutrients in different foods and should therefore also remain compulsory.

4.   Criteria for nutrition claims should be developed

Uniform criteria for nutrition claims throughout the community would be beneficial to consumer understanding and intra-community trade.

5.   There should be definitions for vitamins and minerals, e.g. Vitamin A

It is understood that measurement of Vitamin A has caused barriers to trade with at least one member state not accepting retinol equivalents as a measure of Vitamin A.

6   It should be permitted to give Guideline Daily Amounts

Guideline Daily Amounts (GDAs) are the UK's recommended intake levels for fat and calories by average adults.

7.   Voluntary nutrition information about trans fatty acids should be allowed even if no claim is made

The UK's Committee on Medical Aspects of Food Policy has recommended that, on average, trans fatty acids should provide no more than the current average of about 2% of dietary energy and that consideration should be given to ways of decreasing the amount present in the diet. Separate identification of trans fatty acids would enable people to decrease their consumption.

8.   'Salt' should be allowed in place of 'sodium', or, alternatively, included in brackets after sodium

Many consumers do not understand what sodium is, but are aware of the need to cut down on salt consumption.

9.   The order of the listed nutrients should be changed

The nutrition panel would be more helpful if the order of the nutrients were changed to bring those perceived as most important, e.g. fat, nearer the top of the list.

10.   Additional energy conversion factors

An energy conversion factor of 1kcal/g–5kJ/g for polydextrose should be included. A factor of 4kcal/g should be available for fats in the range 1kcal–4.5kcal/g. These are newly-developed products which, while being 'fats', do not fit the definition of fat.

11.   'Of which' should be changed to 'consisting of'

Consumers do not readily understand the term 'of which'. A more comprehensible term would be 'consisting of'.

12.   Additional comments

- Fibre must be defined and an agreement reached on the method of analysis (*see* 21.6).

- There should be flexibility to require information about additional nutrients if it is felt there is a public health issue.

- Fat and calories per serving should be permitted to be given (or repeated) separately from the nutrition panel.

- It should be permitted to round values to avoid giving an impression of disproportionate precision.

- The vitamin and mineral RDAs should be updated in line with the 31st Report of the EC Scientific Committee for Food.

- Provision should be made to use the term 'Folic acid' instead of 'folacin'.

- There should be provision for vitamins and minerals to be specified if 15% of the RDA is contained within a serving, rather than in 100g/ml.

All of these measures (27.1, 27.2, 27.3), if adopted, would result in an increase in the amount of information required on food labels. With the emphasis on healthy eating, the burgeoning interest in diet and the insistence of consumer organisations that consumers have a right to be given all the relevant details about the food they are purchasing, it seems likely that this trend will continue in the foreseeable future.

APPENDIX 1

Names prescribed by law

(See 4.1)

1. Fish

Species of fish and the names which must be used to describe them are listed in the table below. This does not apply to preserved sardines, tuna and bonito subject to certain EC marketing standards.

A customary name may be used for fish which has been smoked or subjected to a similar process, except for those species marked with an asterisk in the table. In these cases the name used to refer to the smoked fish must be either the name given in the table preceded by the word 'smoked' or, with the exception of *Salmo salar* (L.), 'smoked Pacific salmon'.

Name	Species of fish
Anchovy	All species of *Engraulis*
Bass	*Dicentrarchus labrax* (L.)
Brill	*Scophthalmus rhombus* (L.)
Brisling	*Sprattus sprattus* (L.) when canned
Catfish *or* Rockfish	All species of *Anarhichas*
Cod *or* Codling	*Gadus morhua* (L.) (including *Gadus morhua callarias* and *Gadus morhua morhua*)

Pacific cod *or* cod	*Gadus macrocephalus*
Greenland cod *or* cod	*Gadus ogac*
Coley *or* Saithe *or* Coalfish	*Pollachius virens* (L.)
Conger	All species of *Conger*
Croaker *or* Drum	All species of the family Scianidae
Dab	*Limanda limanda* (L.)
Dogfish *or* Flake *or* Huss *or* Rigg	All species of *Galeorhinus* All species of *Mustelus* All species of *Scyliorhinus* *Galeus melastomas* Rafin. *Squalus acanthias* (L.)
Dory *or* John Dory *or* St Peter's fish	*Zeus faber* (L.)
Eel	All species of *Anguilla*
Emperor	All species of *Lethrinus*
Flounder	*Platichthys flesus* (L.)
Grey mullet	All species of *Mugil* All species of *Liza* All species of *Chelon*
Grouper	All species of *Mycteroperca* All species of *Epinephelus*
Gurnard	All species of the family Triglidae *Peristedion cataphractum* (L.)
Haddock	*Melanogrammus aeglefinus* (L.)
Hake	All species of *Meruccius*
Halibut	*Hippoglossus hippoglossus* (L.) *Hippoglossus stenolepis*
Black halibut	*Reinhardtius hippoglossides* (Walbaum)
Herring	*Clupea harengus* (L.)
Hilsa	*Hilsa elisha*
Hoki	*Macruronus novaezelandiae*

Jack	All species of *Caranx*
	All species of *Hemmicaranx*
	All species of *Seriola*
	All species of *Trachurus*
	All species of *Decapterus*
Ling	All species of *Molva*
Lumpfish *or* Lumpsucker	*Cyclopterus lumpus*
Mackerel	All species of *Scomber*
Megrim	All species of *Lepidorhombus*
Monkfish *or* Angler	*Lophius piscatorius* (L.)
Orange roughy	*Hoplosteppus atlanticus*
Parrot-fish	All species of the family Scaridae
Pilchard	*Sardina pilchardus* (Walbaum)
Pacific pilchard	*Sardinops sagax caerulea* (Girard)
	Sardinops sagax sagax (Jenyns)
	Sardinops sagax melanosticta (Schlegel)
South Atlantic pilchard	*Sardinops sagax ocellata* (Pappe)
Plaice	*Pleuronectes platessa* (L.)
American plaice	*Hippoglossoides platessoides* (Fabr.)
Pollak *or* Pollock *or* Lythe	*Pollachius pollachius* (L.)
Pacific pollack *or* Pacific pollock *or* Alaska pollack *or* Alaska pollock	*Theragra chalcogramma* (Pallas)
Pomfret	All species of *Brama*
	All species of *Stromateus*
	All species of *Pampus*
Redfish *or* Ocean perch *or* Rose fish	All species of *Sebastes*
	Helicolenus maculatus
	Helicolenus dactylopterus (De La Roche)
Red Mullet	All species of *Mullus*
Sardine	Small *Sardina pilchardus* (Walbaum)
Sardinella	All species of *Sardinella*
Sea bream *or* Porgy	All species of the family Sparidae

Sild	Small *Clupea harengus* (L.), when canned
	Small *Sprattus sprattus* (L.), when canned
Skate *or* Ray *or* Roker	All species of *Raja*
Smelt *or* Sparling	All species of *Osmerus*
Sole *or* Dover sole	*Solea solea* (L.)
Lemon sole	*Microstomus kitt* (Walbaum)
Snapper	All species of the family Lutjanidae
Sprat	*Sprattus sprattus* (L.), except when canned
Swordfish	*Xiphias gladius*
Tuna *or* Tunny	All species of *Thunnus*
Skipjack tuna (*or* tuna)	*Euthynnus (Katsuwonus) pelamis*
Albacore tuna (*or* tuna)	*Thunnus alalunga*
Yellowfin tuna (*or* tuna)	*Thunnus (neothunnus) albacores*
Bluefin tuna (*or* tuna)	*Thunnus thynnus*
Bigeye tuna (*or* tuna)	*Thunnus (parathunnus) obesus*
Bonito	All species of *Sarda*
	All species of *Euthynnus*, with the exception of the species *Euthynnus (Katsuwonus) pelamis*
	All species of *Auxis*
Turbot	*Scophthalmus maximus* (L.)
Whitebait	Small *Clupea harengus* (L.) {except when canned}
	Small *Sprattus sprattus* (L.)
Whiting	*Merlangius merlangus* (L.)
Blue whiting	*Micromesistius poutassou* (Risso)
Southern Blue whiting	*Micromesistius australis*
Winter flounder	*Pseudopleuronectes americanus* (Walbaum)
Witch	*Glyptocephalus cynoglossus* (L.)

Salmon and freshwater fish

Catfish	All species of the family Ictaluridae
Carp	All species of the family Cyprinidae
Char	All species of *Salvelinus*
Salmon *or* Atlantic salmon	*Salmo salar* (L.)*
Cherry salmon *or* Pacific salmon	*Oncorhynchus masou* (Walbaum)*
Chum salmon *or* Keta salmon	*Oncorhynchus keta* (Walbaum)*
Medium red salmon *or* Coho salmon *or* Silver salmon	*Oncorhynchus kisutch* (Walbaum)*
Pink salmon	*Oncorhynchus gorbuscha* (Walbaum)*
Red salmon *or* Sockeye salmon	*Oncorhynchus nerka* (Walbaum)*
Spring salmon *or* King salmon *or* Chinook salmon *or* Pacific salmon	*Oncorhynchus tschwytscha* (Walbaum)*
Brown trout *or* trout	*Salmo trutta* (L.) which has spent all its life in fresh water
Sea trout *or* salmon trout	*Salmo trutta* (L.) which has spent all its life in sea water
Cut-throat trout *or* trout	*Oncorhynchus clarkii*
Rainbow trout *or* Steelhead trout *or* trout	*Oncorhynchus mykiss*
Tilapia	All species of *Tilapia*

Shellfish

Abalone *or* Ormer	All species of *Haliotis*
Clam *or* Hard shell clam	{ *Mercenaria mercenaria* (L.) *Venus verrucosa* (L.)
Clam *or* Razor clam	All species of *Ensis* and *Solen*
Cockle	All species of *Cerastoderma*

Crab	{ All species of the section Brachyura All species of the family Lithodidae
Crawfish *or* Spiny lobster *or* Rock lobster	All species of the family Palinuridae *Jasus* spp.
Crayfish	{ All species of the family Astacidae All species of the family Parastacidae All species of the family Austroastacidae
Lobster	All species of *Homarus*
Slipper lobster	All species of *Scyllaridae*
Squat lobster	All species of the family Galatheidae
Mussel	All species of the family Mytulus
Oyster	{ All species of *Crassostrea* All species of *Ostrea*
Oyster *or* Portuguese oyster	*Crassostrea angulata* (Lmk.)
Oyster *or* Pacific oyster	*Crassostrea gigas* (Thunberg)
Oyster *or* Native oyster	*Ostrae edulis* (L.)
King prawn	{ All species of *Penaeus* where the count is less than 123 per kg (head on/shell on) or less than 198 per kg (head off/shell on) or less than 242 per kg (head off/shell off)
Prawn *or* shrimp	{ Whole fish (of a size which, when cooked, have a count of less than 397 per kg) or tails (of a size which, when peeled and cooked, have a count of less than 1,323 per kg) of – all species of *Palaemonidae*, all species of *Penaeidae*, and all species of *Pandalidae*
Shrimp	{ Whole fish (of a size which, when cooked, have a count of 397 per kg or more) or tails (of a size which, when peeled and cooked, have a count of 1,323 per kg or more) of – all species of *Palaemonidae*, all species of *Penaeidae*, and all species of *Pandalidae*

Shrimp *or* Pink shrimp	*Pandalus montagui* (Leach)
Shrimp *or* Brown shrimp	All species of *Crangon*
Scallop	All species of *Pectinidae*
Scallop *or* Queen scallop *or* Queen	*Chlamys (Acquipecton) opercularis* (L.)
Scampi *or* Norway lobster *or* Dublin Bay prawn *or* Langoustine	*Nephrops norvegicus* (L.)
Pacific scampi	*Metanephrops adamanicus* *Metanephrops challengeri*
Tiger prawn	*Penaeus monodon* *Penaeus semisuloalus* *Penaeus esculentus*
Whelk	All species of *Buccinum*
Winkle	All species of *Littorina*

2.   Melons

The name used for melons sold as such must include or be accompanied by an indication of their variety.

3.   Potatoes

The name used for potatoes sold as such must include or be accompanied by an indication of their variety.

4.   Vitamins

The names for vitamins must be as in the table under 18.2. The name for vitamin K must be 'vitamin K'.

Generic names in list of ingredients

(See 6.3)

Generic name	Ingredients	Conditions of use of generic name
Cheese	Any type of cheese or mixture of cheese	The labelling must not refer to a specific type of cheese
Cocoa butter	Press, expeller or refined cocoa butter	
Crumbs *or* rusks, *as appropriate*	Any type of crumbed, baked cereal product	
Crystallised fruit	Any crystallised fruit	The proportion of crystallised fruit must not exceed 10 per cent
Dextrose	Anhydrous dextrose or dextrose monohydrate	
Fat	Any refined fat	The generic name must be accompanied by either: a) the description 'animal' or 'vegetable' as appropriate, or b) an indication of the specific animal origin or the specific vegetable origin of the fat, as appropriate.

		In the case of a hydrogenated fat, the generic name must also be accompanied by the description 'hydrogenated'.
Fish	Any species of fish	The labelling must not refer to a specific species of fish.
Flour	Any mixture of flour derived from two or more cereal species	The generic name must be followed by a list of the cereals from which the flour is derived in descending order of weight
Glucose syrup	Glucose syrup or anhydrous glucose syrup	
Gum base	Any type of gum preparation used in the preparation of chewing gum	
Herb, herbs *or* mixed herbs	Any herb or parts of a herb or combination of two or more herbs or parts of herbs	The proportion of herb or herbs in the food must not exceed 2% by weight
Milk proteins	Any caseins, caseinates or whey proteins, or any mixture of these	
Oil	Any refined oil, other than olive oil	The generic name must be accompanied by either: a) the description 'animal' or 'vegetable' as appropriate, or b) an indication of the specific animal origin or the specific vegetable origin of the oil, as appropriate In the case of a hydrogenated oil, the generic name must also be accompanied by the description 'hydrogenated' (Animal oil includes fish oil.)
Spice, spices *or* mixed spices	Any spice or any combination of two or more spices	The proportion of spice or spices in the food must not exceed 2% by weight

Starch	Any unmodified starch or any starch which has been modified either by physical means or by enzymes	In the case of a starch which may contain gluten, the generic name must be accompanied by an indication of the specific vegetable origin of the starch
Sugar	Any type of sucrose	
Vegetables	Any mixture of vegetables	The proportion of vegetables in the food must not exceed 10% by weight
Wine	Any type of wine defined in Council Regulation (EEC) No. 822/87	

APPENDIX 3

Permitted food additives

Additives permitted by regulations on colours, sweeteners and miscellaneous additives, respectively are listed below, together with their serial numbers (EC numbers). Miscellaneous additives cover the following additive categories: acid, acidity regulator, anti-caking agent, anti-foaming agent, antioxident, bulking agent, carrier, carrier solvent, emulsifier, emulsifying salt, firming agent, flavour enhancer, foaming agent, gelling agent, glazing agent, humectant, modified starch, packaging gas, preservative, propellant, raising agent, sequestrant, stabiliser, thickener.

EC No	Colour
E 100	Curcumin
E 101	(i) Riboflavin
	(ii) Riboflavin-5´-phosphate
E 102	Tartrazine
E 104	Quinoline Yellow
E 110	Sunset Yellow FCF
	Orange Yellow S
E 120	Cochineal, Carminic acid, Carmines
E 122	Azorubine, Carmoisine
E 123	Amaranth
E 124	Ponceau 4R, Cochineal Red A
E 127	Erythrosine

E 128	Red 2G
E 129	Allura Red AC
E 131	Patent Blue V
E 132	Indigotine, Indigo carmine
E 133	Brilliant Blue FCF
E 140	Chlorophylls and Chlorophyllins:
	(i) Chlorophylls
	(ii) Chlorophyllins
E 141	Copper complexes of chlorophylls and chlorophyllins:
	(i) Copper complexes of chlorophylls
	(ii) Copper complexes of chlorophyllins
E 142	Green S
E 150a	Plain caramel
E 150b	Caustic sulphate caramel
E 150c	Ammonia caramel
E 150d	Sulphite ammonia caramel
E 151	Brilliant Black BN, Black PN
E 153	Vegetable carbon
E 154	Brown FK
E 155	Brown HT
E 160a	Carotenes:
	(i) Mixed carotenes
	(ii) Beta-carotene
E 160b	Annatto, bixin, norbixin
E 160c	Paprika extract, capsanthin, capsorubin
E 160d	Lycopene
E 160e	Beta-apo-8´-carotenal (C 30)
E 160f	Ethyl ester of beta-apo-8´-carotenic acid (C 30)
E 161b	Lutein
E 161g	Canthaxanthin
E 162	Beetroot Red, betanin
E 163	Anthocyanins

E 170	Calcium carbonate
E 171	Titanium dioxide
E 172	Iron oxides and hydroxides
E 173	Aluminium
E 174	Silver
E 175	Gold
E 180	Litholrubine BK

EC No	Sweetener
E 420	Sorbitol
	(i) Sorbitol
	(ii) Sorbitol syrup
E 421	Mannitol
E 950	Acesulfame-K
E 951	Aspartame
E 952	Cyclamic acid and its Na and Ca salts
E 953	Isomalt
E 954	Saccharin and its Na, K and Ca salts
E 957	Thaumatin
E 959	Neohesperidine DC
E 965	Maltitol
	(i) Maltitol
	(ii) Maltitol syrup
E 966	Lactitol
E 967	Xylitol

EC No	Miscellaneous additive
E 170	Calcium carbonates
	(i) Calcium carbonate
	(ii) Calcium hydrogen carbonate
E 200	Sorbic acid
E 202	Potassium sorbate
E 203	Calcium sorbate
E 210	Benzoic acid
E 211	Sodium benzoate
E 212	Potassium benzoate
E 213	Calcium benzoate
E 214	Ethyl p-hydroxybenzoate
E 215	Sodium ethyl p-hydroxybenzoate
E 216	Propyl p-hydroxybenzoate
E 217	Sodium propyl p-hydroxybenzoate
E 218	Methyl p-hydroxybenzoate
E 219	Sodium methyl p-hydroxybenzoate
E 220	Sulphur dioxide
E 221	Sodium sulphite
E 222	Sodium hydrogen sulphite
E 223	Sodium metabisulphite
E 224	Potassium metabisulphite
E 226	Calcium sulphite
E 227	Calcium hydrogen sulphite
E 228	Potassium hydrogen sulphite
E 230	Biphenyl, diphenyl
E 231	Orthophenyl phenol
E 232	Sodium orthophenyl phenol
E 233	Thiabendazole
E 234	Nisin

E 235	Natamycin
E 239	Hexamethylene tetramine
E 242	Dimethyl dicarbonate
E 249	Potassium nitrite
E 250	Sodium nitrite
E 251	Sodium nitrate
E 252	Potassium nitrate
E 260	Acetic acid
E 261	Potassium acetate
E 262	Sodium acetates
	(i) Sodium acetate
	(ii) Sodium hydrogen acetate (sodium diacetate)
E 263	Calcium acetate
E 270	Lactic acid
E 280	Propionic acid
E 281	Sodium propionate
E 282	Calcium propionate
E 283	Potassium propionate
E 284	Boric acid
E 285	Sodium tetraborate (borax)
E 290	Carbon dioxide
E 296	Malic acid
E 297	Fumaric acid
E 300	Ascorbic acid
E 301	Sodium ascorbate
E 302	Calcium ascorbate
E 304	Fatty acid esters of ascorbic acid
	(i) Ascorbyl palmitate
	(ii) Ascorbyl stearate
E 306	Tocopherol-rich extract
E 307	Alpha-tocopherol
E 308	Gamma-tocopherol

E 309	Delta-tocopherol
E 310	Propyl gallate
E 311	Octyl gallate
E 312	Dodecyl gallate
E 320	Butylated hydroxyanisole (BHA)
E 321	Butylated hydroxytoluene (BHT)
E 322	Lecithins
E 325	Sodium lactate
E 326	Potassium lactate
E 327	Calcium lactate
E 330	Citric acid
E 331	Sodium citrates
	(i) Monosodium citrate
	(ii) Disodium citrate
	(iii) Trisodium citrate
E 332	Potassium citrates
	(i) Monopotassium citrate
	(ii) Tripotassium citrate
E 333	Calcium citrates
	(i) Monocalcium citrate
	(ii) Dicalcium citrate
	(iii) Tricalcium citrate
E 334	Tartaric acid (L(+)-)
E 335	Sodium tartrates
	(i) Monosodium tartrate
	(ii) Disodium tartrate
E 336	Potassium tartrates
	(i) Monopotassium tartrate
	(ii) Dipotassium tartrate
E 337	Sodium potassium tartrate
E 338	Phosphoric acid

E 339	Sodium phosphates
	(i) Monosodium phosphate
	(ii) Disodium phosphate
	(iii) Trisodium phosphate
E 340	Potassium phosphates
	(i) Monopotassium phosphate
	(ii) Dipotassium phosphate
	(iii) Tripotassium phosphate
E 341	Calcium phosphates
	(i) Monocalcium phosphate
	(ii) Dicalcium phosphate
	(iii) Tricalcium phosphate
E 350	Sodium malates
	(i) sodium malate
	(ii) Sodium hydrogen malate
E 351	Potassium malate
E 352	Calcium malates
	(i) Calcium malate
	(ii) Calcium hydrogen malate
E 353	Metatartaric acid
E 354	Calcium tartrate
E 355	Adipic acid
E 356	Sodium adipate
E 357	Potassium adipate
E 363	Succinic acid
E 380	Triammonium citrate
E 385	Calcium disodium ethylene diamine tetra-acetate (calcium disodium EDTA)
E 400	Alginic acid
E 401	Sodium alginate
E 402	Potassium alginate
E 403	Ammonium alginate

E 404	Calcium alginate
E 405	Propane-1,2-diol alginate
E 406	Agar
E 407	Carrageenan
E 407a	Processed eucheuma seaweed
E 410	Locust bean gum
E 412	Guar gum
E 413	Tragacanth
E 414	Acacia gum (gum arabic)
E 415	Xanthan gum
E 416	Karaya gum
E 417	Tara gum
E 418	Gellan gum
E 420	Sorbitol
	(i) Sorbitol
	(ii) Sorbitol syrup
E 421	Mannitol
E 422	Glycerol
E 431	Polyoxyethylene stearate
E 432	Polyoxyethylene sorbitan monolaurate (polysorbate 20)
E 433	Polyoxyethylene sorbitan monooleate (polysorbate 80)
E 434	Polyoxyethylene sorbitan monopalmitate (polysorbate 40)
E 435	Polyoxyethylene sorbitan monostearate (polysorbate 60)
E 436	Polyoxyethylene sorbitan tristearate (polysorbate 65)
E 440	Pectins
	(i) Pectin
	(ii) Amidated pectin
E 442	Ammonium phosphatides
E 444	Sucrose acetate isobutyrate
E 445	Glycerol esters of wood rosins

E 450   Diphosphates

                        (i)   Disodium diphosphate

                        (ii)   Trisodium diphosphate

                        (iii) Tetrasodium diphosphate

                        (iv)   Dipotassium diphosphate

                        (v)   Tetrapotassium diphosphate

                        (vi)   Dicalcium diphosphate

                        (vii) Calcium dihydrogen diphosphate

E 451   Triphosphates

                        (i)   Pentasodium triphosphate

                        (ii) Pentapotassium triphosphate

E 452   Polyphosphates

                        (i)   Sodium polyphosphate

                        (ii)   Potassium polyphosphate

                        (iii)   Sodium calcium polyphosphate

                        (iv) Calcium polyphosphates

E 460   Cellulose

                        (i) Microcrystalline cellulose

                        (ii) Powdered cellulose

E 461   Methyl cellulose

E 463   Hydroxypropyl cellulose

E 464   Hydroxypropyl methyl cellulose

E 465   Ethyl methyl cellulose

E 466   Carboxy methyl cellulose

                  Sodium carboxy methyl cellulose

E 470a   Sodium, potassium and calcium salts of fatty acids

E 470b   Magnesium salts of fatty acids

E 471   Mono- and diglycerides of fatty acids

E 472a   Acetic acid esters of mono- and diglycerides of fatty acids

E 472b   Lactic acid esters of mono- and diglycerides of fatty acids

E 472c   Citric acid esters of mono- and diglycerides of fatty acids

E 472d   Tartaric acid esters of mono- and diglycerides of fatty acids

E 472e	Mono- and diacetyl tartaric acid esters of mono- and diglycerides of fatty acids
E 472f	Mixed acetic and tartaric acid esters of mono- and diglycerides of fatty acids
E 473	Sucrose esters of fatty acids
E 474	Sucroglycerides
E 475	Polyglycerol esters of fatty acids
E 476	Polyglycerol polyricinoleate
E 477	Propane-1, 2-diol esters of fatty acids
E 479b	Thermally oxidised soya bean oil interacted with mono- and diglycerides of fatty acids
E 481	Sodium stearoyl-2-lactylate
E 482	Calcium stearoyl-2-lactylate
E 483	Stearyl tartrate
E 491	Sorbitan monostearate
E 492	Sorbitan tristearate
E 493	Sorbitan monolaurate
E 494	Sorbitan monooleate
E 495	Sorbitan monopalmitate
E 500	Sodium carbonates
	(i) Sodium carbonate
	(ii) Sodium hydrogen carbonate
	(iii) Sodium sesquicarbonate
E 501	Potassium carbonates
	(i) Potassium carbonate
	(ii) Potassium hydrogen carbonate
E 503	Ammonium carbonates
	(i) Ammonium carbonate
	(ii) Ammonium hydrogen carbonate
E 504	Magnesium carbonates
	(i) Magnesium carbonate
	(ii) Magnesium hydroxide carbonate (syn.: Magnesium hydrogen carbonate)

E 507	Hydrochloric acid
E 508	Potassium chloride
E 509	Calcium chloride
E 511	Magnesium chloride
E 512	Stannous chloride
E 513	Sulphuric acid
E 514	Sodium sulphates

    (i) Sodium sulphate

    (ii) Sodium hydrogen sulphate

E 515	Potassium sulphates

    (i) Potassium sulphate

    (ii) Potassium hydrogen sulphate

E 516	Calcium sulphate
E 517	Ammonium sulphate
E 520	Aluminium sulphate
E 521	Aluminium sodium sulphate
E 522	Aluminium potassium sulphate
E 523	Aluminium ammonium sulphate
E 524	Sodium hydroxide
E 525	Potassium hydroxide
E 526	Calcium hydroxide
E 527	Ammonium hydroxide
E 528	Magnesium hydroxide
E 529	Calcium oxide
E 530	Magnesium oxide
E 535	Sodium ferrocyanide
E 536	Potassium ferrocyanide
E 538	Calcium ferrocyanide
E 541	Sodium aluminium phosphate, acidic
E 551	Silicon dioxide
E 552	Calcium silicate

E 553a	(i) Magnesium silicate
	(ii) Magnesium trisilicate
E 553b	Talc
E 554	Sodium aluminium silicate
E 555	Potassium aluminium silicate
E 556	Calcium aluminium silicate
E 558	Bentonite
E 559	Aluminium silicate (Kaolin)
E 570	Fatty acids
E 574	Gluconic acid
E 575	Glucona-delta-lactone
E 576	Sodium gluconate
E 577	Potassium gluconate
E 578	Calcium gluconate
E 579	Ferrous gluconate
E 585	Ferrous lactate
E 620	Glutamic acid
E 621	Monosodium glutamate
E 622	Monopotassium glutamate
E 623	Calcium diglutamate
E 624	Monoammonium glutamate
E 625	Magnesium diglutamate
E 626	Guanylic acid
E 627	Disodium guanylate
E 628	Dipotassium guanylate
E 629	Calcium guanylate
E 630	Inosinic acid
E 631	Disodium inosinate
E 632	Dipotassium inosinate
E 633	Calcium inosinate
E 634	Calcium 5′-ribonucleotides
E 635	Disodium 5′-ribonucleotides

E 640	Glycine and its sodium salt
E 900	Dimethyl polysiloxane
E 901	Beeswax, white and yellow
E 902	Candelilla wax
E 903	Carnauba wax
E 904	Shellac
E 912	Montan acid esters
E 914	Oxidised polyethylene wax
E 927b	Carbamide
E 938	Argon
E 939	Helium
E 941	Nitrogen
E 942	Nitrous oxide
E 948	Oxygen
E 950	Acesulfame-K
E 951	Aspartame
E 953	Isomalt
E 957	Thaumatin
E 959	Neohesperidine DC
E 965	Maltitol
	(i) Maltitol
	(ii) Maltitol syrup
E 966	Lactitol
E 967	Xylitol
E 999	Quillaia extract
E 1200	Polydextrose
E 1201	Polyvinylpyrrolidone
E 1202	Polyvinylpolypyrrolidone
E 1404	Oxidised starch
E 1410	Monostarch phosphate
E 1412	Distarch phosphate
E 1413	Phosphated distarch phosphate

E 1414	Acetylated distarch phosphate
E 1420	Acetylated starch
E 1422	Acetylated distarch adipate
E 1440	Hydroxy propyl starch
E 1442	Hydroxy propyl distarch phosphate
E 1450	Starch sodium octenyl succinate
E 1505	Triethyl citrate
E 1518	Glyceryl triacetate (triacetin)

APPENDIX 4

Additive references in ingredients lists

According to MAFF, the following criteria should be used when deciding how to identify additives in ingredients lists.

Additive numbers

Where the serial number of the additive is to be given in the ingredients list

- the number used should be one which appears in the column headed 'EC No.' in Appendix 3 (e.g. 'E150b', 'E420', 'E553a').

Additive names

Where the specific name of the additive is to be given in the ingredients list

- the name used should be one which appears in the column headed 'Colour' or 'Sweetener' or 'Miscellaneous additive' in Appendix 3 (e.g. 'Cochineal', 'Carminic acid' or 'Carmines'; 'Aspartame'; 'Magnesium silicate' or 'Magnesium trisilicate'.

- a summary name which appears in the column headed 'Colour' or 'Sweetener' or 'Miscellaneous additive' in Appendix 3 may be used in place of a more specific name provided that the latter do not have their own serial numbers (e.g. 'carotene' may be used for 'mixed carotenes'; 'sorbitol' may be used for 'sorbitol syrup'; 'sodium citrate' may be used for 'disodium citrate'; 'potassium phosphate' may be used for 'tripotassium phosphate').

- if the name in the column headed 'Colour' or 'Sweetener' or 'Miscellaneous additive' in Appendix 3 is preceded by a bracketed letter or Roman numeral (e.g. '(ii) Beta carotene'; '(i) Sorbitol'; '(i) Monosodium citrate'), this need not be given as part of the name.

- in the case of miscellaneous additives, where an alternative to the specific name is given in brackets in the column headed 'Miscellaneous additives' in Appendix 3, this may be used in place of the specific name (e.g. 'polysorbate 20' instead of 'Polyoxyethylene sorbitan monolaurate').

- in the case of miscellaneous additives being phosphates, the names 'Diphosphates', 'Triphosphates' and 'Polyphosphates' are acceptable as specific names for the phosphates covered by the serial numbers E450, E451 and E452 respectively. They should not be used for the phosphates covered by serial numbers E338, E339, E340 and E341.

- synonyms or acronyms which are not included in the relevant schedule should *not* be used as alternatives to the specific name.

APPENDIX 5

Foods that should carry a 'use by' date

Foods which need labelling with 'use by' dates are those that have to be stored at low temperatures to maintain their safety rather than their quality. They will have a short product life following manufacture, after which their consumption may present a risk of food poisoning. They will be likely to fall into one or both of the following groups:

• foods which at ambient or chill temperatures are capable of supporting the formation of toxins or multiplication of pathogens to a level which could lead to food poisoning if they are not stored correctly;

• foods intended for consumption either without cooking or after treatment (such as reheating) unlikely to be sufficient to destroy food poisoning organisms which may be present.

Types of food which fall into these categories are as follows:

Dairy products

• Soft or semi-hard cheese ripened by moulds and/or bacteria once the ripening or maturation is completed;

• Dairy-based desserts (including milk substitutes), such as fromage frais, mousses, creme caramels, products containing whipped cream;

unless the pH of the product would prevent the growth of pathogenic micro-organisms or the formation of toxins, or other effective preservative mechanisms are present.

Cooked products

- Products, including sandwiches, containing or comprising cooked meat, poultry, fish, eggs (or substitutes for meat, poultry, fish or eggs), milk, hard and soft cheese, cereals (including rice), pulses, and vegetables whether or not they are intended to be eaten without further reheating.

Smoked or cured ready to eat meat which is not shelf-stable at room temperature

- including sliced cured cooked meats such as hams, some salamis and other fermented sausages, depending on the method of curing.

Prepared ready-to-eat foods

- Including prepared vegetables, vegetable salads containing fruit, or prepared salads (such as coleslaw) containing other products and prepared products such as mayonnaise.

Uncooked or partly cooked pastry and dough products

- Including pizzas, sausage rolls or fresh pasta, containing meat, poultry, fish (or substitutes of meat, poultry or fish) or vegetables.

Uncooked products

- Uncooked products comprising or containing either meat, poultry or fish.

Vacuum or modified atmosphere packs

- Foods packed in a vacuum or modified atmosphere and held at chill temperatures to keep them safe.

Certain foods, such as bread and many cakes, deteriorate over a short period in quality rather than safety. They do not, therefore, need a 'use by' date. Chilled foods which do not support the growth of food poisoning organisms, e.g. butter and margarines, do not need a 'use by' date.

Foods which would normally need a 'use by' date but which are sold to the consumer frozen should not be given a 'use by' date.

APPENDIX 6

Recommendations of the Advisory Committee on the Microbiological Safety of Food

Certain recommendations relating to food labelling are given below.

We recommend that industry label **cheese made from raw milk** from cows and other species so that consumers can identify it.

We recommend that industry label **raw minced beef and minced beef products** with appropriate handling and cooking instructions.

We recommend that industry should ensure that the cooking instructions supplied with **beefburgers** should be capable of achieving an internal temperature of 70°C for 2 minutes (or equivalent), so that the burger's juices run clear, and there are no pink bits inside.

In relation to **raw, flash-fried poultry products**, industry should introduce more informative labelling, in order to make clear to consumers that such products require thorough cooking.

APPENDIX 7

UK regulations relevant to the text

The Food Labelling Regulations 1996, SI 1996/1499

The Food Labelling (Amendment) Regulations 1998, SI 1998/1398

The Colours in Food Regulations 1995, SI 1995/3124

The Sweeteners in Food Regulations 1995, SI 1995/3123, as amended by SI 1996/1477 and SI 1997/814

The Miscellaneous Food Additives Regulations 1995, SI 1995/3187, as amended by SI 1997/1413

The Meat Products and Spreadable Fish Products Regulations 1984, SI 1984/1566, as amended by SI 1986/987

The Food (Lot Marking) Regulations 1996, SI 1996/1502

The Weights and Measures (Packaged Goods) Regulations 1986, SI 1986/2049 as amended by SI 1994/1852

The Weights and Measures (Miscellaneous Foods) Order 1988, SI 1988/2040

The Weights and Measures (Quantity Marking and Abbreviation of Units) Regulations 1987, SI 1987/1538, as amended by SI 1988/627 and SI 1994/1851

The Milk and Milk Products (Protection of Designations) Regulations 1990, SI 1990/607

The Organic Products Regulations 1992, SI 1992/2111, as amended by SI 1993/405, SI 1994/2286 and SI 1997/166

The Novel Foods and Novel Food Ingredients Regulations 1997, SI 1997/1335